10/11

Postmodernism: A Very Short Introduction

'the most intellectually incisive, coherent and comprehensive meditation upon the history and significance of postmodernism that I have yet encountered.'
Patricia Waugh, University of Durham

'easily the best introduction to postmodernism currently available.'
Hans Bertens, Utrecht University

VERY SHORT INTRODUCTIONS are for anyone wanting a stimulating and accessible way in to a new subject. They are written by experts, and have been published in more than 25 languages worldwide.

The series began in 1995, and now represents a wide variety of topics in history, philosophy, religion, science, and the humanities. Over the next few years it will grow to a library of around 200 volumes – a Very Short Introduction to everything from ancient Egypt and Indian philosophy to conceptual art and cosmology.

Very Short Introductions available now:

ANCIENT PHILOSOPHY
  Julia Annas
THE ANGLO-SAXON AGE
  John Blair
ANIMAL RIGHTS   David DeGrazia
ARCHAEOLOGY   Paul Bahn
ARCHITECTURE
  Andrew Ballantyne
ARISTOTLE   Jonathan Barnes
ART HISTORY   Dana Arnold
ART THEORY   Cynthia Freeland
THE HISTORY OF
  ASTRONOMY   Michael Hoskin
ATHEISM   Julian Baggini
AUGUSTINE   Henry Chadwick
BARTHES   Jonathan Culler
THE BIBLE   John Riches
BRITISH POLITICS
  Anthony Wright
BUDDHA   Michael Carrithers
BUDDHISM   Damien Keown
CAPITALISM   James Fulcher
THE CELTS   Barry Cunliffe
CHOICE THEORY
  Michael Allingham
CHRISTIAN ART   Beth Williamson
CLASSICS   Mary Beard and
  John Henderson
CLAUSEWITZ   Michael Howard
THE COLD WAR
  Robert McMahon

CONTINENTAL PHILOSOPHY
  Simon Critchley
COSMOLOGY   Peter Coles
CRYPTOGRAPHY
  Fred Piper and Sean Murphy
DADA AND SURREALISM
  David Hopkins
DARWIN   Jonathan Howard
DEMOCRACY   Bernard Crick
DESCARTES   Tom Sorell
DRUGS   Leslie Iversen
THE EARTH   Martin Redfern
EGYPTIAN MYTHOLOGY
  Geraldine Pinch
EIGHTEENTH-CENTURY
  BRITAIN   Paul Langford
THE ELEMENTS   Philip Ball
EMOTION   Dylan Evans
EMPIRE   Stephen Howe
ENGELS   Terrell Carver
ETHICS   Simon Blackburn
THE EUROPEAN UNION
  John Pinder
EVOLUTION
  Brian and Deborah Charlesworth
FASCISM   Kevin Passmore
THE FRENCH REVOLUTION
  William Doyle
FREUD   Anthony Storr
GALILEO   Stillman Drake
GANDHI   Bhikhu Parekh

GLOBALIZATION
  Manfred Steger
HEGEL   Peter Singer
HEIDEGGER   Michael Inwood
HINDUISM   Kim Knott
HISTORY   John H. Arnold
HOBBES   Richard Tuck
HUME   A. J. Ayer
IDEOLOGY   Michael Freeden
INDIAN PHILOSOPHY
  Sue Hamilton
INTELLIGENCE   Ian J. Deary
ISLAM   Malise Ruthven
JUDAISM   Norman Solomon
JUNG   Anthony Stevens
KANT   Roger Scruton
KIERKEGAARD   Patrick Gardiner
THE KORAN   Michael Cook
LINGUISTICS   Peter Matthews
LITERARY THEORY
  Jonathan Culler
LOCKE   John Dunn
LOGIC   Graham Priest
MACHIAVELLI   Quentin Skinner
MARX   Peter Singer
MATHEMATICS   Timothy Gowers
MEDIEVAL BRITAIN
  John Gillingham and
  Ralph A. Griffiths
MODERN IRELAND
  Senia Pašeta
MOLECULES   Philip Ball
MUSIC   Nicholas Cook
NIETZSCHE   Michael Tanner
NINETEENTH-CENTURY
  BRITAIN   Christopher Harvie and
  H. C. G. Matthew
NORTHERN IRELAND
  Marc Mulholland
PAUL   E. P. Sanders
PHILOSOPHY   Edward Craig
PHILOSOPHY OF SCIENCE
  Samir Okasha

PLATO   Julia Annas
POLITICS   Kenneth Minogue
POLITICAL PHILOSOPHY
  David Miller
POSTCOLONIALISM
  Robert Young
POSTMODERNISM
  Christopher Butler
POSTSTRUCTURALISM
  Catherine Belsey
PREHISTORY   Chris Gosden
PRESOCRATIC PHILOSOPHY
  Catherine Osborne
PSYCHOLOGY   Gillian Butler and
  Freda McManus
QUANTUM THEORY
  John Polkinghorne
ROMAN BRITAIN   Peter Salway
ROUSSEAU   Robert Wokler
RUSSELL   A. C. Grayling
RUSSIAN LITERATURE
  Catriona Kelly
THE RUSSIAN REVOLUTION
  S. A. Smith
SCHIZOPHRENIA
  Chris Frith and Eve Johnstone
SCHOPENHAUER
  Christopher Janaway
SHAKESPEARE   Germaine Greer
SOCIAL AND CULTURAL
  ANTHROPOLOGY
  John Monaghan and Peter Just
SOCIOLOGY   Steve Bruce
SOCRATES   C. C. W. Taylor
SPINOZA   Roger Scruton
STUART BRITAIN   John Morrill
TERRORISM   Charles Townshend
THEOLOGY   David F. Ford
THE TUDORS   John Guy
TWENTIETH-CENTURY
  BRITAIN   Kenneth O. Morgan
WITTGENSTEIN   A. C. Grayling
WORLD MUSIC   Philip Bohlman

Available soon:

AFRICAN HISTORY
  John Parker and Richard Rathbone
ANCIENT EGYPT   Ian Shaw
THE BRAIN   Michael O'Shea
BUDDHIST ETHICS
  Damien Keown
CHAOS   Leonard Smith
CHRISTIANITY   Linda Woodhead
CITIZENSHIP   Richard Bellamy
CLASSICAL ARCHITECTURE
  Robert Tavernor
CLONING   Arlene Judith Klotzko
CONTEMPORARY ART
  Julian Stallabrass
THE CRUSADES
  Christopher Tyerman
DERRIDA   Simon Glendinning
DESIGN   John Heskett
DINOSAURS   David Norman
DREAMING   J. Allan Hobson
ECONOMICS   Partha Dasgupta
THE END OF THE WORLD
  Bill McGuire
EXISTENTIALISM   Thomas Flynn
THE FIRST WORLD WAR
  Michael Howard
FREE WILL   Thomas Pink
FUNDAMENTALISM
  Malise Ruthven
HABERMAS   Gordon Finlayson

HIEROGLYPHS
  Penelope Wilson
HIROSHIMA   B. R. Tomlinson
HUMAN EVOLUTION
  Bernard Wood
INTERNATIONAL RELATIONS
  Paul Wilkinson
JAZZ   Brian Morton
MANDELA   Tom Lodge
MEDICAL ETHICS
  Tony Hope
THE MIND   Martin Davies
MYTH   Robert Segal
NATIONALISM   Steven Grosby
PERCEPTION   Richard Gregory
PHILOSOPHY OF RELIGION
  Jack Copeland and Diane Proudfoot
PHOTOGRAPHY
  Steve Edwards
THE RAJ   Denis Judd
THE RENAISSANCE
  Jerry Brotton
RENAISSANCE ART
  Geraldine Johnson
SARTRE   Christina Howells
THE SPANISH CIVIL WAR
  Helen Graham
TRAGEDY   Adrian Poole
THE TWENTIETH CENTURY
  Martin Conway

For more information visit our web site

www.oup.co.uk/vsi

Christopher Butler

POST-MODERNISM

A Very Short Introduction

OXFORD
UNIVERSITY PRESS

OXFORD

UNIVERSITY PRESS

Great Clarendon Street, Oxford OX2 6DP

Oxford University Press is a department of the University of Oxford.
It furthers the University's objective of excellence in research, scholarship,
and education by publishing worldwide in

Oxford New York

Auckland Bangkok Buenos Aires Cape Town Chennai
Dar es Salaam Delhi Hong Kong Istanbul Karachi Kolkata
Kuala Lumpur Madrid Melbourne Mexico City Mumbai Nairobi
São Paulo Shanghai Taipei Tokyo Toronto

Oxford is a registered trade mark of Oxford University Press
in the UK and in certain other countries

Published in the United States
by Oxford University Press Inc., New York

© Christopher Butler 2002

The moral rights of the author have been asserted
Database right Oxford University Press (maker)

First published as a Very Short Introduction 2002

British Library Cataloguing in Publication Data

Data available

Library of Congress Cataloging in Publication Data

Data available

ISBN 978-0-19-280239-2

13 15 17 19 20 18 16 14

Typeset by RefineCatch Ltd, Bungay, Suffolk
Printed in Great Britain by
Ashford Colour Press Ltd, Gosport, Hampshire

Contents

List of illustrations   viii

1   The rise of postmodernism   1

2   New ways of seeing the world   13

3   Politics and identity   44

4   The culture of postmodernism   62

5   The 'postmodern condition'   110

References   129

Further reading   133

Index   135

List of illustrations

1 Interior of Westin
   Bonaventure Hotel by
   Portman   4
   John Portman & Associates

2 Ray Federman, *Take It
   or Leave It : A Novel*
   (1976)   22
   Fiction Collective, New York

3 Untitled film still (1977)
   by Cindy Sherman   54
   © Cindy Sherman/Metro
   Pictures

4 Untitled film still (1978)
   by Cindy Sherman   54
   © Cindy Sherman/Metro
   Pictures

5 *Fool's House* (1962) by
   Jasper Johns   63
   © Jasper Johns/VAGA, New
   York/DACS, London 2002. Leo
   Castelli Gallery, New York

6 *New Hoover Quadraflex*
   (1981–6) by Jeff Koons 65
   © Jeff Koons Productions Inc.

7 *SS Amsterdam in Front of
   Rotterdam* (1966) by
   Malcolm Morley   77
   © Malcolm Morley. Norman and
   Irma Braman collection. Courtesy
   of Sperone Westwater, New York

8 Holland Hotel by
   Richard Estes   79
   © Richard Estes. Marlborough
   Gallery, New York

9 *Early One Morning*
   (1962) by Anthony
   Caro   82
   © Anthony Caro. Photo © Tate,
   London 2002

10 *An Oak Tree* (1973) by
   Michael Craig-Martin 83
   © Michael Craig-Martin.
   Australian National Gallery,
   Canberra

11 *Picture for Women*
   (1979) by Jeff Wall   86
   © Jeff Wall. Musée national d'art
   moderne, Paris. Photo © RMN

12   Sainsbury Wing, National
     Gallery, London (1991) by
     Venturi, Scott Brown and
     Associates   90
     © Martin Charles

13   Theatre of Abraxas by
     Ricardo Bofill   91
     © Charles Jencks

14   *The Dinner Party* (1979)
     by Judy Chicago   96
     © ARS, NY and DACS, London
     2002. Judy Chicago
     collection. Photo © Donald
     Woodmann

15   *Interior Scroll* (1975) by
     Carolee Schneeman   98
     © ARS, NY and DACS, London
     2002. Photo © Anthony McCall

16   *Untitled, #228* (1990)
     by Cindy Sherman   99
     © Cindy Sherman/Metro Pictures

17   *Untitled (Your gaze hits
     the side of my face)* (1981)
     by Barbara Kruger   101
     © Barbara Kruger. Mary Boone
     Gallery, New York

18   *Her Story* (1984) by
     Elizabeth Murray   107
     © Elizabeth Murray.
     Pace Wildenstein, New York

19   *Grandma and the
     Frenchman (Identity
     Crisis)* (1990) by
     Robert Colescott   108
     © Robert Colescott. Phyllis Kind
     Gallery, New York

20   *The Imagineers Main
     Street USA* (1955)
     Anaheim, California   113
     From Ghirardo, *Architecture after
     Modernism* (1996) © Bettmann/
     Corbis

21   *Odalisk* (1955–8) by
     Robert Rauschenberg 124
     © Robert Rauschenberg/DACS,
     London/VAGA, New York 2002.
     Museum Ludwig Köln. Photo ©
     Rheinisches Bildarchiv

The publisher and the author apologize for any errors or omissions in the above list. If contacted they will be pleased to rectify these at the earliest opportunity.

Chapter 1
The rise of postmodernism

Carl Andre's rectangular pile of bricks, *Equivalent* VIII (1966), annoyed lots of people when shown at the Tate Gallery, London, in 1976. It is a typically postmodernist object. Now re-enshrined in the Tate Modern, it doesn't resemble much in the canon of modernist sculpture. It is not formally complex or expressive, or particularly engaging to look at, indeed it can soon be boring. It is easy to repeat. Lacking any features to sustain interest in itself (except perhaps to Pythagorean number mystics) it inspires us to ask questions about its context rather than its content: 'What is the point of this?', or 'Why is this displayed in a museum?' Some theory about the work has to be brought in to fill the vacuum of interest, and this is also fairly typical. It might inspire the question 'Is it really art, or just a heap of bricks pretending to be art?' But this is not a question that makes much sense in the postmodernist era, in which it seems to be generally accepted that it is *the institution* of the gallery, rather than anything else, which has made it, *de facto*, a 'work of art'. The visual arts just are what museum curators show us, from Picasso to sliced-up cows, and it is up to us to keep up with the ideas surrounding these works.

Many postmodernists (and of course their museum director allies) would like us to entertain such thoughts about the ideas which might surround this 'minimalist' art. A pile of bricks is designedly elementary; it confronts and denies the emotionally expressive qualities of previous (modernist) art. Like Duchamp's famous *Urinal* or his bicycle wheel mounted on a stool, it tests our intellectual responses and our tolerance of the works that the art gallery can bring to the attention of its public. It makes some essentially critical points, which add up to some quite self-denying assumptions about art. Andre says: 'What I try to find are sets of particles and the rules which combine them in the simplest way', and claims that his equivalents are 'communistic because the form is equally accessible to all men'.

This sculpture, however politically correct it may be interpreted to be, isn't nearly as *enjoyable* as Rodin's *Kiss*, or the far more intricate abstract structures of a sculptor like Anthony Caro. Andre's theoretical avant-gardism, which tests our intellectual responses, suggests that the pleasures taken in earlier art are a bit suspect. Puritanism, 'calling into question', and making an audience feel guilty or disturbed, are all intimately linked by objects like this. They are attitudes which are typical of much postmodernist art, and they often have a political dimension. The artwork for which Martin Creed won the Turner Prize in 2001 continues this tradition. It is an empty room, in which the electric lights go on and off.

I will be writing about postmodernist artists, intellectual gurus, academic critics, philosophers, and social scientists in what follows, as if they were all members of a loosely constituted and quarrelsome political party. This party is by and large internationalist and 'progressive'. It is on the left rather than the right, and it tends to see everything, from abstract painting to personal relationships, as political undertakings. It is not particularly unified in doctrine, and even those who have most significantly contributed ideas to its manifestos sometimes indignantly deny membership – and yet the postmodernist party tends to believe that its time has come. It is certain of its uncertainty, and often claims that it has seen through the sustaining illusions of others, and so has grasped the 'real' nature of the cultural and political institutions which surround us. In doing this, postmodernists often follow Marx. They claim to be peculiarly aware of the unique state of contemporary society, immured as it is in what they call 'the postmodern condition'.

Postmodernists therefore do not simply support aesthetic 'isms', or avant-garde movements, such as minimalism or conceptualism (from which work like Andre's bricks emerged). They have a distinct way of seeing the world as a whole, and use a set of philosophical ideas that not only support an aesthetic but also analyse a 'late capitalist' cultural condition of 'postmodernity'. This condition is supposed to affect us all, not just through avant-garde art, but also at a more fundamental level, through the influence of that huge growth in media communication by electronic means which Marshall McLuhan in the 1960s called the 'electronic village'. And yet in our new 'information society', paradoxically enough, most information is apparently to be distrusted, as being more of a contribution to the manipulative image-making of those in power than to the advancement of knowledge. The postmodernist attitude is therefore one of a suspicion which can border on paranoia (as seen, for example, in the conspiracy-theory novels of Thomas Pynchon and Don DeLillo, and the films of Oliver Stone).

A major Marxist commentator on postmodernism, Frederic Jameson, sees Jon Portman's Westin Bonaventura Hotel in Los Angeles as entirely symptomatic of this condition. Its extraordinary complexities of entranceways, its aspiration towards being 'a complete world, a kind of miniature city', and its perpetually moving elevators, make it a 'mutation' into a 'postmodernist hyperspace' which transcends the capacities of the human body to locate itself, to find its own position in a mappable world. This 'milling confusion', says Jameson, is a dilemma, a 'symbol and analogue' of the 'incapacity of our minds . . . to map the great global multinational and decentred communicational network in which we find ourselves caught as individual subjects'. Many of us have felt something like this in London's Barbican Centre.

This 'lost in a big hotel' view of our condition shows postmodernism

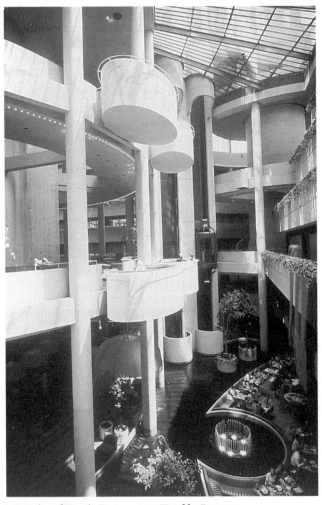

1. Interior of Westin Bonaventure Hotel by Portman.
'Postmodernist hyperspace'.

to be a doctrine for the metropolis, within which a new climate of ideas has arisen and brought with it a new sensibility. But these ideas and attitudes have always been very much open to debate, and in what follows I shall combat postmodernist scepticism with some of my own. Indeed, I will deny that its philosophical and political views and art forms are nearly as dominant as a confident proclamation of a new 'postmodernist' era might suggest.

It is nevertheless obvious by now that even if we restrict ourselves to the ideas current within the artistic avant-garde since 1945, we can sense a break with those of the modernist period. The work of James Joyce is very different from that of Alain Robbe-Grillet, that of Igor Stravinsky from that of Karlheinz Stockhausen, that of Henri Matisse from that of Robert Rauschenberg, of Jean Renoir from that of Jean-Luc Godard, of Jacob Epstein from that of Carl Andre, and of Mies van der Rohe from that of Robert Venturi. What one makes of this contrast between the modern and the postmodern in the arts largely depends on the values one embraces. There is no single line of development to be found here.

Many of these differences arose from the sensitivity of artists to changes in the climate of ideas. By the mid-1960s, critics like Susan Sontag and Ihab Hassan had begun to point out some of the characteristics, in Europe and in the United States, of what we now call postmodernism. They argued that the work of postmodernists was deliberately less unified, less obviously 'masterful', more playful or anarchic, more concerned with the processes of our understanding than with the pleasures of artistic finish or unity, less inclined to hold a narrative together, and certainly more resistant to a certain interpretation, than much of the art that had preceded it. We will look at some examples of this later on.

The rise of theory

Somewhat later than the period in which the artists mentioned above established themselves, a further postmodernist development took place: 'the rise of theory' among intellectuals and academics. Workers in all sorts of fields developed an excessively critical self-consciousness. Postmodernists reproached modernists (and their supposedly 'naive' liberal humanist readers or spectators or listeners) for their belief that a work of art could somehow appeal to all humanity, and so be free of divisive political implications.

The rise of the great post-war innovatory artists – Stockhausen, Boulez, Robbe-Grillet, Beckett, Coover, Rauschenberg, and Beuys – was succeeded (and many would say supplemented and explained) by the huge growth in the influence of a number of French intellectuals, notably the Marxist social theorist Louis Althusser, the cultural critic Roland Barthes, the philosopher Jacques Derrida, and the historian Michel Foucault, all of whom in fact began their work by thinking about the implications of modernism, and rarely had any very extended relationship to the contemporary avant-garde. Althusser was concerned with Brecht; Barthes with Flaubert and Proust; Derrida with Nietzsche, Heidegger, and Mallarmé; and Foucault with Nietzsche and Bataille. By the mid-1970s it becomes difficult to know what matters most to postmodernists – the fashioning of a particular kind of (disturbing) experience within art, or the new philosophical and political interpretative opportunities which it offered. Many would now say that for committed postmodernists, interpretative implications were always (and disastrously) 'privileged' over the enjoyable artistic embodiment and formal sophistication which so many had learned to appreciate in modernist art.

This startlingly new framework of ideas was exported from the France of the late 1960s and early 1970s into England, Germany, and the United States. By the time of the student uprisings of 1968, the most advanced philosophical thought had moved away from the strongly ethical and individualist existentialism that was typical of the immediately post-war period (of which Sartre and Camus were the best-publicized exponents) towards far more sceptical and anti-humanist attitudes. These new beliefs were expressed in what came to be known as deconstructive and poststructuralist theory, to be discussed below. The 'new novelists' in France also moved away from an interest in the philosophico-emotional states of angst and absurdity, and a commitment to the mimetic engagements of a traditionally narrated novel, such as Sartre's *La Nausée* or Camus's *La Peste* and *L'Étranger*, towards a far colder, contradiction-filled anti-narrative method in the texts of Alain Robbe-Grillet, Philippe Sollers, and others, who were not so much interested in individual character, or coherent narrative suspense and interest, as in the play of their own authorial language.

The new ideas, although they came to inspire some literature, and to dominate its interpretation in academic circles, were actually rooted outside the arts. Barthes was mainly interested in the application of linguistic models to the interpretation of text, Derrida's philosophical work began as a critique of linguistics, and Foucault's base was in the social sciences and history. They were also all guided to a greater or lesser degree by the re-reading or redemption of Marx (whose dominance in places like the Soviet Union was, before 1989, rather airily explained away as due to a misapplied 'bureaucratic socialism'). Most of the French intellectuals responsible for the theoretical inspiration of postmodernism worked within a broadly Marxist paradigm.

Postmodernist doctrines thus drew upon a great deal of philosophical, political, and sociological thought, which disseminated itself into the artistic avant-garde (particularly in the visual arts) and into the humanities departments of universities in Europe and the United States as 'theory'. The postmodernist period is one of the extraordinary dominance of the work of academics over that of artists.

This was not 'theory' as it might be understood in the philosophy of science (in which theories are tested, and so verifiable or falsifiable) or in Anglo-American, broadly empiricist philosophy. It was a far more self-involved, sceptical type of discourse which adapted

7

general concepts derived from traditional philosophy to literary, sociological, or other material, which was thereby given a postmodernist twist.

Lost in translation?

Many academic proponents of postmodernist theory in England and the United States therefore concentrated on the inward translation of Continental thought. This led to a number of interestingly transplanted cultural concerns, and a sharp break with previous traditions. For example, postmodernist theory inherited a concern for the functions of language from structuralism, but when Jacques Derrida turned his attention to the problem of reference (of language to external non-linguistic reality) he went back to the linguist Ferdinand de Saussure. Derrida struggled with him (in *De la grammatologie*) apparently in blissful ignorance of the fact that many of the problems which concerned him, and the (very slippery) position he himself came to, had, in the opinion of many in the philosophical community (even in France), been far better stated and more rigorously analysed by Ludwig Wittgenstein. But Derrida does not mention Wittgenstein in his early work. Many Derridean literary theorists were therefore seriously ignorant of the history of philosophical problems, and were unaware of some of the standard solutions to them in the Anglo-American philosophical tradition. This led to intellectual division, mutual incomprehension, and splits in many university departments that persist to this day.

Postmodernists, who were rightly enthusiasts for 'liberating' ethical and political doctrines, were at the same time immensely dependent on the extraordinary prestige of these new intellectual authorities, whose influence was not a little sustained by their heavy reliance upon a neologizing jargon, which imparted a tremendous air of difficulty and profundity to their deliberations and caused great difficulties to their translators. According to the American philosopher John Searle:

Michel Foucault once characterised Derrida's prose style to me as *'obscurantisme terroriste'*. The text is written so obscurely that you can't figure out exactly what the thesis is (hence *'obscurantisme'*) and then when one criticises this, the author says, *'Vous m'avez mal compris; vous êtes idiot'* (hence *'terroriste'*).

New York Review of Books, 27 October 1983

The often obscure, not to say obfuscating, modes of speech and writing of these intellectuals were sometimes even intended to signify a defiance of that 'Cartesian' clarity of exposition which they said arose from a suspect reliance upon 'bourgeois' certainties concerning the world order. Roland Barthes, discussing 17th-century French literature, says that:

> Doubtless there was a certain universality of writing which stretched across to the elite elements of Europe living the same privileged life-style, but this much-prized communicability of the French language has been anything but horizontal; it has never been vertical, never reached the depths of the masses.

Roland Barthes, *Oeuvres Complètes* vol. I (1942–65)

A suggestive punning word-play was preferred to a plodding and politically suspect logic, and the result was a theory which was more literary than philosophical, and which rarely if ever came to clear or empirically testable conclusions, simply because it was so difficult to be sure about what it meant. This placed a very satisfying burden of translation exposition and defence upon the followers of the masters of theory. The French masters wrote in a resolutely avant-gardist way against the clarity of their own national tradition. It is the thousands of echoes and adaptations, and unsurprising misunderstandings, of their obscure writings that have made up the often confused and pretentious collective psyche of the postmodernist constituency.

Here is an example of a far from untypical sentence, which won the second prize in the annual Bad Writing Contest promoted by the scholarly journal *Philosophy and Literature*. It may or may not become clearer to the reader by the end of this book, and it comes from Homi Bhabha's much referred to *The Location of Culture* (1994).

> If, for a while, the ruse of desire is calculable for the uses of discipline, soon the repetition of guilt, justification, pseudo-scientific theories, superstition, spurious authorities and classification can be seen as the desperate effort to 'normalise' normally the disturbance of a discourse of splitting that violates the rational enlightened claims of its enunciatory modality.

There is therefore a great contrast and tension between the postmodernism which derived from French intellectuals and the main stream of Anglo-American liberal philosophical thought in this period. The latter tradition had been very suspicious, in a post-Orwellian manner, of jargon, of grandiose synthesis, and of Marxist-derived 'ideology'. In the 1960s and early 1970s it was much wedded to very different methods, and most particularly to the idea that philosophy should work within an 'ordinary language' accessible to all, and even when technical aim at maximum clarity. The typical work of philosophy in English, from Gilbert Ryle's *The Concept of Mind* (1949) through to John Rawls's *A Theory of Justice* (1971), used these methods to ask for an essentially cooperative and consensual method, and for further clarification and piecemeal correction by the philosophy profession as a whole (to which, indeed, the original authority might well respond, as did Rawls in his later *Political Liberalism*, 1993). In this it was as much influenced by the model of scientific cooperation as by Socratic methods. But postmodernist ideas, despite their Marxist affiliations and political aspirations, were never intended to fit into anything like this kind of consensual and cooperative framework. Many postmodernists thought that this would have simply reproduced a bourgeois view of the world, and aimed at an unjustifiable universal acceptance. There is a sense in which French postmodernism is a true successor to the surrealist movement, which also tried to disrupt supposedly 'normal' ways of seeing things.

The danger, but also the point, for many postmodernists, of embedding theoretical and philosophical arguments within a literary rhetoric is that the text is thereby left open to all sorts of interpretations. There is as we shall see a deep irrationalism at the heart of postmodernism – a kind of despair about the Enlightenment-derived public functions of reason – which is not to be found elsewhere in the other developing intellectual disciplines of the late 20th century (for example, in the influence of cognitive science on linguistics, or the use of Darwinian models to explain mental development). Books of a postmodernist persuasion are often advertised by their publishers, not for their challenging hypotheses or arguments, but for their *use* of theory', their 'insights', their 'interventions', their 'addressing' (rather than answering) questions.

Some broad distinctions between the philosophy and ethics, the aesthetics, and the political sociology of postmodernism structure the account which follows. In all three areas the criteria for being postmodern vary a good deal: the very term 'postmodernist' draws attention to a mixture of historical period and ideological implications. The claim of any work of art or thinker or social practice to typify postmodernist doctrines, or to diagnose with accuracy 'the social condition of postmodernity', will therefore depend on the very diverse criteria that have held sway in the minds of most commentators on the subject, including my own. I nevertheless hope that in what follows I will capture a broad consensual view of postmodernism.

I will introduce the most important of the large family of ideas involved, but cannot, in the space available, pay too much attention to the intriguing disputes between them. I concentrate on what seem to me to have been the most viable and long-lived postmodernist ideas, and especially those that can help us to characterize and understand the innovative art and cultural practices of the period since the mid-1960s.

We should be prepared to see many postmodernist ideas as very interesting and influential, and as the key to some good experimental art – but at best confused, and at worst simply untrue. This is not unusual – the essential leading ideas of many cultural epochs are open to the same criticism. Once found out, such ideas are either reinterpreted (like the Romantic idea of Imagination) or just condemned to obsolescence (like the idea of mesmerism in medicine). All extremist intellectual movements in history have this character, and postmodernism is one of them. No one now subscribes entirely to the Romantic view of Imagination, even though the functions of the imagination have remained an abiding and central concern. And 18th-century mesmerism and 20th-century hypnotism are very different from one another. The rise of radical ideas (as of radical political parties) in the 20th century has generally led to disillusion followed by modification, and this seems already to be the fate of postmodernism, from the 1960s to the 1990s. After all, it has already lasted as long as the high modernism of the period before the war – of which it is, for those in favour of it, the politically progressive replacement, and for those against it, the last decadent gasp.

Chapter 2

New ways of seeing the world

Resisting grand narratives

A great deal of postmodernist theory depends on the maintenance of a sceptical attitude: and here the philosopher Jean-François Lyotard's contribution is essential. He argued in his *La condition postmoderne* (published in French in 1979, in English in 1984) that we now live in an era in which legitimizing 'master narratives' are in crisis and in decline. These narratives are contained in or implied by major philosophies, such as Kantianism, Hegelianism, and Marxism, which argue that history is progressive, that knowledge can liberate us, and that all knowledge has a secret unity. The two main narratives Lyotard is attacking are those of the progressive emancipation of humanity – from Christian redemption to Marxist Utopia – and that of the triumph of science. Lyotard considers that such doctrines have 'lost their credibility' since the Second World War: 'Simplifying to the extreme, I define *postmodern* as incredulity towards metanarratives'.

These metanarratives traditionally serve to give cultural practices some form of legitimation or authority. (The legitimation of Marxist or Freudian theories thus would stem from their claim, not widely accepted by now, that they are based on the principles or metanarrative of science.) Another example of this would be the textbook history of the writing of the Constitution of the United

States, by the Founding Fathers, along with its subsequent legislative enactments. This grand historical narrative with its constitutional 'founding principles' is still very much a going concern in current disputes in the United States about the limits of free speech, the right to abortion, and the right of American private citizens to bear arms. Another simple example of metanarrative is the Marxist belief in the predestined and privileged function of the proletariat, with the party as its ally, in bringing about a revolution, and in the Utopia which is supposed to follow, when 'the state has withered away'. In the period since 1945, the governments of many formerly colonized territories have developed similarly would-be masterful political narratives about the history of nationalist struggle. It is difficult to avoid such narratives, and nearly all nation-states have them.

Although there are good liberal reasons for being *against* such 'grand narratives' (on the grounds that they do not allow for disputes about value, and often enough lead to totalitarian persecution), the plausibility of Lyotard's claim for the decline of metanarratives in the late 20th century ultimately depends upon an appeal to the cultural condition of an intellectual minority. The general *sociological* claim that such narratives are in decline in our period looks pretty thin, even after the collapse of state-sponsored Marxism in the West, because allegiances to large-scale, totalizing religious and nationalist beliefs are currently responsible for so much repression, violence, and war – in Northern Ireland, Serbia, the Middle East, and elsewhere. (Postmodernists tend not to be well informed about current practices in science and religion.) It is obvious to any reader of the newspapers that men and women are still more or less willing to kill one another in the name of grand narratives every day – think of the *fatwa* against Salman Rushdie. Indeed, the reason why academic postmodernists seemed so secure in their hostile analysis of the American and European societies around them in the 1970s may well have derived from the fact that these societies were not torn apart by contrary ideologies. Some thoughts about the rival claims of Islam and Judaism in the Middle

East, or of Marxism and the democratic process in Eastern Europe, might have led to different conclusions. But the scepticism about commitments to master narratives promoted by Lyotard, and echoed by Derrida and many other postmodernists, had a strong appeal to a generation brought up in Western democracies. They were liberated to some degree from theology by existentialism, impressed by the resistance offered to capitalism and the military-industrial complex in 1968, suspicious of American 'imperialist' pretensions, and perhaps more importantly needed to escape the deadeningly Manichaean ideological platitudes of the Cold War period.

The result was that the basic attitude of postmodernists was a scepticism about the claims of any kind of overall, totalizing explanation. Lyotard was not alone in seeing the intellectual's task as one of 'resistance', even to 'consensus', which 'has become an outmoded and suspect value'. Postmodernists responded to this view, partly for the good reason that by doing so they could side with those who didn't 'fit' into the larger stories – the subordinated and the marginalized – against those with the power to disseminate the master narratives. Many postmodernist intellectuals thus saw themselves as avant-garde and bravely dissentient. This heralded a pluralist age, in which, as we shall see, even the arguments of scientists and historians are to be seen as no more than quasi narratives which compete with all the others for acceptance. They have no unique or reliable fit to the world, no certain correspondence with reality. They are just another form of fiction.

Of course, an opposition to such narratives (particularly holistic or totalitarian ones) is an absolutely traditional liberal concern. Much significant postmodernist writing has therefore turned on articulating this kind of scepticism for essentially liberal ends, as for example in the work of Edward Said, who in his *Orientalism* (1978) attempted to show the distorting effects of the projection of the Western grand narrative of imperialism upon Oriental societies. For the imperialist saw himself as the representative of a rational, ordered, peaceful, and law-abiding framework, and defined the Orient as the opposite of this (for example, as the 'muddle' Forster found in *A Passage to India*), and had the confidence that his representation of 'them' – his narrative of 'Orientalism' – would prevail. The grand imperial story of progressive development was superimposed on a merely local – and, what is more, 'deviant' – Oriental practice. In all this Said follows Foucault, and the Euhemerism of the Greeks and of Nietzsche, in believing that such imposing political grand narratives are at best mystificatory attempts to keep some social groups in power, and others out of it. As Said notes, when Flaubert slept with an Egyptian courtesan, Kuchuk Hanem, he wrote to Louise Colet that 'the oriental woman is no more than a machine; she makes no distinction between one man and another man'. In so doing (and in his subsequent novels) he 'produced a widely influential model of the Oriental woman'. But within this influential narrrative, 'she never spoke of herself, never represented her emotions, presence or history.' We can imagine how different her own account might indeed have been, but the two frameworks for narrative, Flaubert's and Kuchuk Hanem's, seem to be culturally incommensurable; hence a typical postmodernist conclusion, that universal truth is impossible, and relativism is our fate.

Deconstruction

The confidence with which such claims were made was influenced to a huge degree by a reading of the philosophy of Jacques Derrida, in whose voluminous writings the most elaborate version of this 'deconstructive' attitude was to be found.

The central argument for deconstruction depends on relativism, by which I mean the view that truth itself is always relative to the differing standpoints and predisposing intellectual frameworks of the judging subject. It is difficult to say, then, that deconstructors are committed to anything as definite as a philosophical thesis. Indeed, to attempt to define deconstruction is to defy another of its main principles – which is to deny that final or true definitions are possible, because even the most plausible candidates will always invite a further defining move, or 'play', with language. For the deconstructor, the relationship of language to reality is not given, or even reliable, since all language systems are inherently unreliable cultural constructs.

Derrida and his followers nevertheless seem to be committed to one fairly clear historical proposition: that philosophy and literature in the Western tradition had for too long falsely supposed that the relationship between language and world was, on the contrary, well founded and reliable. (And even, for some religions, guaranteed by God.) This false 'logocentric' confidence in language as the mirror of nature is the illusion that the meaning of a word has its origin in the structure of reality itself and hence makes the truth about that structure directly present to the mind. All this amounts to a false 'metaphysics of presence'. This is Derrida's own grand metanarrative, and he seems quite falsely to assume that there was nothing in the Western metaphysical philosophical tradition which put into question the fit of language to the world – but nominalism and essentialism have long been at odds. (In fact, Wittgenstein had notoriously tried to work out an absolutely stable and reliable relationship of language to world in his *Tractatus Logico-Philosophicus* (1922) and then had completely repudiated its position in favour of a theory of relativistically related language games by the time of the (posthumous) publication of his *Philosophical Investigations* in 1953.)

Nevertheless, as a disobliging characterization of a culture that had come increasingly to rely on such claims to a 'good fit' in science and in the all-conquering capitalist technology which was supposed to flow from it and justify it, Derrida's scepticism had a considerable political appeal. It allowed his followers to attack those who believed that philosophy, science, or the novel really did describe the world accurately, or that a historical narrative can be true.

Literary people in particular were accused by Derrideans of a naive trust in what was ironically dubbed the 'classic realist text'. Such persons simply fail to appreciate the nature of the language from which they derive their false confidence.

In reading George Eliot's *Middlemarch* (1882), for example, we may have the illusion (not actually shared by George Eliot) that she simply opens a window upon reality, and that her discourse is fully adequate to a description of the real. Our reliance upon Eliot's narrative voice and language puts us in a dominating, even God-like position, especially if we rely upon the generalizations that she makes. So we think we know the truth about Dorothea Brooke, when all we really know is Eliot's descriptions of her, and, in any case, what happens when we come across a metaphor – are they 'true' too? To give an example, Dorothea, bewildered and distressed by her experience of Casaubon's unsatisfactoriness as a husband, thinks that her life 'seemed to have become *a masque with enigmatical costumes*'. Quite apart from the problems of interpreting the metaphor, it will only work within a culture in which masques and their functions are understood in a certain way. The description of Dorothea is only valid within, and so relative to, the masque-appreciating discourse which is current within a certain group.

The postmodernist deconstructor wishes then to show how a previously trusted relationship, like this one between language and the world, will go astray. 'Look' we say, 'it's just a systematically misleading metaphor about a masque.' However, it is logically obvious that you can't demonstrate how language always 'goes astray' without *at the same time* having a secret and contradictory trust in it. For without a pretty confident notion of the truth, how can we show that any particular stretch of language has 'gone astray' or fallen into contradiction? This is a crippling mystery to those hostile to deconstruction, and a sustaining one to those who practise its faith.

Why, then, should deconstructors wish to call into question our reliance on authors like Eliot, and with her much of the previous philosophical tradition?

Signs as systems

Derrideans insisted that all words must be explained only in terms of their relationships to the various systems in which they take part. It follows that we are at best relativists, caught within (incommensurable) conceptual systems. We can only 'know' what *they* permit us to know about reality. Whatever we say, we are caught within a linguistic system that does not relate to external reality in the way we expect, because every term within each system also alludes to, or depends upon, the existence (or, as Derrida put it, the 'trace') of other terms within the system that are absent. For example, English has a family of words for degrees of anger – from 'irritated' to 'furious'. And French has its own, different, family for this area of our experience. All the terms within each language's family rely upon one another to divide up the field of 'anger' for native speakers. But neither system, English or French, different as they clearly are, can fairly claim to finally encode the 'truth' about states of anger in the world. Nor can Eliot claim to finally encode the truth about Dorothea's disillusionment. For Derrideans then, language only seems to mark out clear differences between concepts; it actually only 'defers', or pushes away, its partners within the system for a while. Our concepts thus mark, for Derrideans, a '*différance*', or a deferring of meaning, just as much as they signify a difference (the French neologism puns between the two). For meaning perpetually slips away from word to word within the linguistic chain.

Derrida goes on from this venerable form of conceptual relativism to suggest ways in which all conceptual frameworks, once seen this way, can be criticized. This is his key contribution to the postmodernist attitude, and it doesn't much depend on the 'correctness' or otherwise of his philosophical position. For he sees all conceptual systems as prone to a falsifying, distorting, *hierarchization*. Not only is our knowledge of the world not as direct as we like to believe – metaphor-ridden and entirely relative to the scope of our conceptual systems – but we have been all too confident about the ways in which the central categories within those systems work to organize our experience. For example, George Eliot clearly relies in the passage to which I alluded on a clear distinction between 'appearance' and 'reality', and between people 'being themselves' and merely 'acting' (as in a masque or wearing a disguise).

We tend to 'privilege', or rely upon, what Derrida calls particular 'transcendental signifiers', such as 'God', 'reality', the 'idea of man', to organize our discourse. The conceptual oppositions we tend to employ to do this organization for us – speech versus writing, soul versus body, literal versus metaphorical, natural versus cultural, masculine versus feminine – make us get lots of fundamental relationships wrong, or at least too rigidly fixed. In particular, we tend to put one of these terms above the other, so that, for example, 'woman' is thought of as inferior to 'man' ('Oriental' inferior to 'Western'). But within a more relativistic conceptual scheme, we can see that they 'really' depend on one another for their definition. Indeed, it was a very Freudian obsession of Derrideans that apparent opposites really need one another, and always imply one another. I can only see myself as a rational, justice-seeking imperialist (like Forster's Ronnie Fielding) *if* you are at the same time to be seen as a wily, slippery, muddled Oriental (like Forster's Aziz). The innovatory, liberating aspect of this type of deconstruction of oppositions works in this way: when we look at particular systems like this, which purport to describe the world correctly, we can see that the concepts they 'privilege' or make central, and the hierarchies they order them into, are not nearly so certainly in the 'right' order, and are much more interdependent, than we thought.

For Derrideans, indeed, the revelation of their hidden interdependence 'deconstructs' them. They can be undone or reversed, often to paradoxical effect, so that truth is 'really' a kind of fiction, reading is always a form of *mis*reading, and, most fundamentally, understanding is always a form of *mis*understanding, because it is never direct, is always a form of partial interpretation, and often uses metaphor when it thinks it is being literal. It is this central use of deconstruction to subvert our confidence in logical, ethical, and political commonplaces that has proved most revolutionary – and typical of postmodernism.

For the relativist claim is that once we see our conceptual systems in this way, we can also see that the world, its social systems, human identity even, are not *givens*, somehow guaranteed by a language which corresponds to reality, but are *constructed by us* in language, in ways that can never be justified by the claim that this is the way that such things 'really are'. We live, not inside reality, but inside our representations of it. (In a notorious Derridean aside – 'there is nothing outside the text', only the *more* text that we use to try to describe or analyse that to which texts purport to refer.)

All this can give us the confidence to break away from an allegiance to any 'given' systems, and to believe that the way we see the world can and should be changed. Deconstructors, liberals, and Marxists can all get into some kind of alliance here, in denying that any dominant ideology, or post-Enlightenment, Kantian, universalizing, or imperialist language, can really describe the way things are.

Playing with the text

Deconstruction (particularly as practised by literary critics) was culturally most influential when it refused to allow an intellectual activity, or a literary text, or its interpretation, to be organized by any customary hierarchy of concepts, and particularly those exemplified above. In performing these tasks deconstruction disrupted the text's organization, and contested what it saw as merely 'arbitrary' delimitations of its meanings. This was because

I know what you guys are going to come up with next And what about representation? Yes what about it? Correct strict representation of reality! Words sticking to things! Meaning sticking to words! (Signifiant / Signifié), exact use of GRAMMATOLOGY (coucou) in order to differentiate speaking from writing and shouting from mumbling!

Yes I know what you think of writing and that for you guys it's an important (crucial) question, but we've already discussed all that and me in a sense (in LA LOGIQUE DU SENS if you wish) I don't give a damn about THE ORDER OF THINGS because me, I do not relate, I do not narrate, I do not recite in order to create order, rather not!

On the contrary what I do has to do with the problem of reading or listening. And not L' E C R I T U R E ! Me I speak to the senses and I'm not trying to make sense in any way. I deal in nonsense I deal in S U R F I C T I O N ! Or if you prefer I'm working my way toward unreadability, toward free reading, delirious reading, in a way I'm in favor of reading in flagrant breach of peace, caught in the act: F L A G R A N-T E D E L I C T O ! I don't fuck around!
But okay I'll stop this crap (single space, double space, triple space) and all that typographical masturbation. To tell the truth it disgusts me just as much as it might disgust you. But sometimes it is necessary to talk (or even write) about such things. Just to situate the problem correctly.

Yes, but what happens to language, you might ask?
What happens to meaning?
Good question!

2. From Ray Federman, *Take It or Leave It : A Novel* (1976).
The play of postmodernist fiction with theory is best when it is also comic.

the '*differance*', or semi-concealed dependence of one concept on others in its family, is illimitable. We could travel right through the dictionary on the pathways opened up by one word. This notion of a dynamically inter-related, potentially unlimited language field, helped to ally deconstructive theory to the experimental attitudes of many avant-gardist, postmodernist writers. The 'new novelists' in France and a number of American experimental writers, such as Walter Abish, Donald Barthelme, Robert Coover, and Ray Federman, were influenced by such ideas. The language and conventions of texts (and pictures and music) became something to *play* with – they were not committed to delimited arguments or narratives. They were the mere *disseminators* of 'meanings'.

The Death of the Author

Most importantly, the reader/listener/spectator involved in the articulation or interpretation of this play of language should act independently of any supposed intentions of the author. Attention to an author would privilege quite the wrong thing, for seeing him or her as an origin, or a delimiting authority, for the meaning of the text was an obvious example of the (logocentric) privileging of a particular set of meanings. Why should these not originate in the reader just as much as the author? Authorial (or historical) intention should no more be trusted than realism. There thus arose a new notion of the text, as a 'free play of signs within language'. This proclamation of 'The Death of the Author', notably by Barthes and Foucault, also had the political advantage of doing away with him or her as the bourgeois, capitalist, owner and marketer of his or her meanings.

As Barthes put it:

> We know now that a text is not a line of words releasing a single 'theological' meaning (the 'message of the Author-God') but a multidimensional space in which a variety of writings, none of them

original, blend and clash ... Literature ... by refusing to assign a
'secret', an ultimate meaning, to the text, (and to the world as text)
liberates what may be called an anti-theological activity, an activity
that is truly revolutionary since to refuse to fix meaning is in the end
to refuse God and his hypostasis – reason, science, law.

Roland Barthes, 'The Death of the Author', in
Image-Music-Text (1977)

The text, as really constructed by the reader, was thereby
liberated and democratized for the free play of the imagination.
Meanings became the property of the interpreter, who was free
to play, deconstructively, with them. It was thought to be both
philosophically wrong and politically retrogressive to attempt
to determine the meaning of a text, or any semiotic system, to
particular ends. All texts were now liberated to swim, with
their linguistic or literary or generic companions, in a sea of
intertextuality in which previously accepted distinctions
between them hardly mattered, and to be seen collectively as
forms of playful, disseminatory rhetoric (rather like Derrida's
own lectures, which became freewheeling, disorganized,
unfocused, lengthy monologues). The pursuit of verbal
certainties in interpretation was thought to be as reactionary
in its implications as was the manufactured consensus of the
established political order.

Metaphor

The plausibility of this way of seeing texts as forms of
(deconstructable) rhetorical play, however truth-telling in
intention, was greatly reinforced by the thesis, inherited from
Nietzsche and a reading of Plato, that right through language
(including the most 'realistic' parts of George Eliot) *the apparently
literal is also really metaphorical*. Philosophy and history (neither
any longer to be privileged as literal, or truth-telling, discourses)
can be read as if they were literature, and vice versa. We need no
longer believe in the literal (as a kind of language referring

unambiguously to reality) because all candidates for the literal can be shown to be metaphorical when more closely analysed.

This view of language in general has met with a growing acceptance from many linguists, notably as led, not uncontroversially, by George Lakoff and Mark Johnson, who acknowledge the influence of Derrida in seeing the whole of everyday language as organized by metaphor. To that extent they too are inclined to argue that a philosophically 'objectivist' view of the world is untenable. Such linguistic work has attempted to show that we actually think, every day, through interlocking conceptual systems based on metaphors, which cannot be reduced in any way to a 'more literal' language and so are very unlikely to be simply or systematically compatible with one another.

It was the political and ethical consequences of this kind of analysis that were of interest to postmodernists in general. For the deconstructors had maintained that all systems of thought, once seen as metaphorical, inevitably led to contradictions or paradoxes or impasses or '*aporias*', to use the Derridean word (which is the rhetorical term for a dubitative question). This is because for Derrideans the metaphorical characteristics of a language system will always ensure that it actually fails to command (or master) the subject matter which it purports to explain.

These arguments enchanted a very large number of literary critics in the 1970s and early 1980s, and they still do. For deconstruction of this kind was an avant-garde, sceptical, contradiction-revealing strategy, which could undermine, subvert, expose, 'undo', and transgress any text. What is more, it had exciting political implications, since it showed the indubitable superiority of the deconstructor's 'insights' to the text's unwitting 'blindness' to the contradictions it encoded. To deconstruct a poem, text, or discourse is to show how it (actually) undermines the philosophy it (seems to) assert, or the hierarchical oppositions on which it overtly relies. And deconstruction was most effective when the

contradictions it thus revealed were of moral or political
importance.

Here is a rather rough example of a deconstructive approach, based
on part of a poem by the young Tennyson, who writes of his:

> Reverèd Isabel, the crown and head,
> The stately flower of female fortitude,
> Of perfect wifehood and pure lowlihead.
>
> II
> The intuitive decision of a bright
> And thorough-edged intellect to part
> Error from crime; a prudence to withhold;
> The laws of marriage charactered in gold
> Upon the blanched tablets of her heart;
> A love still burning upward, giving light
> To read those laws; an accent very low
> In blandishment, but a most silver flow
> Of subtle-paced counsel in distress,
> Right to the heart and brain, though undescried,
> Winning its way with extreme gentleness
> Through all the outworks of suspicious pride;
> A courage to endure and to obey;
> A hate of gossip parlance, and of sway,
> Crowned Isabel, through all her placid life,
> The queen of marriage, a most perfect wife.

This is meant to praise, in fulsomely religiose language, but the
topics chosen to reinforce these strategies can be seen to be,
within our own historical context, objectionable. And the
deconstructor can say that their inadequacy to *our* sense of reality
(or rather to political correctness) will derive from the fact that
they are really based on fantasy, that is on an uneasy relationship
between the literal and the metaphorical in the poem. They will
reveal within themselves, if we look carefully, an unease about the

very distinctions on which they trade. And so the poem will fall apart.

For a highly objectionable dominance of men over women is disguised (and made acceptable, to men at least) by the pretence that women can indeed 'reign' over men – but only in morally acceptable ways. They have the virtue, we have the power. But virtue, particularly of the peculiarly self-abnegating kind praised by Tennyson, isn't a power at all. It is allowed to arise only in a metaphorical (rather than a literal, marriage) context in which women are powerless: hence the unfortunate conjunction of 'perfect wifehood and pure lowlihead'. What is more, Isabel can use her intelligence only *intuitively* when dividing error from crime (reinforcing the old opposition, women are intuitive and men reasonable). And just in case her intuition lets her down, she carries the Moses-like 'laws of marriage' around with her as an *aide-memoire*, which is furthermore 'charactered' on the pure, blank 'blanched tablets of her heart'. Even her heart is white, bloodless, and empty: she is indeed a *tabula rasa* for male fantasy. Even the love she feels is allowed to do little more than engender 'light / to read those laws'. Her only weapons in 'distress' are gentleness, and a courage which is significantly tempered by obedience. She doesn't want 'sway', and yet she is god-like, since there is no harm in a worship that doesn't directly confront sexual differences. Tennyson's poem, paradoxically and to its own deconstruction, subordinates Isabel while praising her to the skies.

In arguing that language can lead us astray in this way, and that 'reality' can never be wholly or convincingly mastered, deconstruction refuses to accept the possibility of any sustained *realism* in the texts it attacks. This attack on realism is absolutely central to all types of postmodernist activity. But in refusing to come inside any existing system, or to make any exposition of one, in anything but a playful or evasive manner, it also has to deny the possibility of proposing a system of its own, without betraying its own premises. Hence the accusation frequently made against deconstructor postmodernists, that they are just sceptics who cannot make significant moral or political commitments. Deconstructors too often, true to their own premises, tangle themselves up in a perpetual regress of qualification. Much deconstructive criticism (for example, Geoffrey Hartman's *Glas* and much of the work of Paul de Man and Hillis Miller) now seems to be self-indulgent and self-absorbed, and ultimately uncommitted to anything that matters.

Those examples of deconstructive interpretation that are most convincing in fact arbitrarily arrest this playful regress for the purpose of standing by a thesis that isn't, at least immediately, being criticized. Out-and-out deconstructors can never quite get away from the accusation that their work is at best a form of pragmatic criticism of our beliefs, and is in the end in the same old philosophical business of pointing out, not so much that if you contradict yourself, you haven't said anything (which would for them be far too much tied to a literal, traditional, truth-telling logic), as that if you contradict yourself, you open up all sorts of interesting pathways for exploration. After all, according to them, we will all inevitably do this, and the only possible response to that is to make another move in the game, not to be so bold as to rule out some moves as simply illegitimate. Traditional deconstruction is not so much a testable theory, then, as a continuing 'project'.

Scepticism and ideology

Deconstruction, deeply academic and self-involved though it mostly was, supported a general move towards relativist principles in postmodernist culture. It left postmodernists not particularly interested in empirical confirmation and verification in the sciences. They often saw this as contaminated by an association with the military-industrial complex, the use of a rigid technological rationality for social control, and so on. It also meant that the followers of Lyotard and Derrida tended to believe in 'stories' rather than in testable theories. Postmodernists, having abandoned their belief in traditional ('realistic') philosophy, history, and science under the influence of French thought, thus became more and more the theorizers of the (delusive) workings of *culture*, and that is why most of my examples of the application of the philosophical and political ideas of postmodernism are drawn from the arts.

Postmodernist thought sees the culture as containing a number of perpetually competing stories, whose effectiveness depends not so much on an appeal to an independent standard of judgement, as upon their appeal to the communities in which they circulate – like rumour in Northern Ireland. As Seyla Benhabib points out, for Lyotardians:

> Transcendental guarantees of truth are dead; in the agonal struggle of language games there is no commensurability; there are no criteria of truth transcending local discourses, but only the endless struggle of local narratives vying with one another for legitimation.
> Seyla Benhabib, *Situating the Self* (1992)

Postmodernism thus involved a highly critical epistemology, hostile to any overarching philosophical or political doctrine, and strongly opposed to those 'dominant ideologies' that help to maintain the status quo.

Nevertheless, many postmodernists allied the Derridean style of critique to a more constructively subversive ideology. They saw that pointing out an unwitting allegiance to a contradictory position (like that of Tennyson) was very much what Marx and Freud had been up to. Marx had maintained that workers are in a state of 'false consciousness': they assent to the bourgeois proposition that they are giving their labour *freely* as autonomous individuals to the market, but they are really imprisoned by economically determined structures of class antagonism. This was known with certainty to Marxist theorists of this period (and in very non-Derridean terms) as 'real power relations'. Freudians could similarly argue that the conflict between the superego (conforming to socially sanctioned beliefs) and unconscious secret or repressed desires (for example, for sexual expression) would inevitably lead to internal contradictions, which are open to a Derridean reading. And so, paradoxically enough, in concentrating on the notion of hidden contradiction, many postmodernists allied themselves to two highly disputable, and certainly totalizing, 19th-century ideologies.

Of course, it is possible to point out such ideology-undoing internal contradictions without claiming at the same time to have an alternative overall solution to society's problems. One can analyse contradictions to point to social tension without implicitly offering a general Marxist or Freudian solution, simply by promoting the thesis discussed above, that all language systems will be found to contain contradictions because they are essentially metaphorical. Not surprisingly, this aspect of postmodernism appealed immensely to literary and cultural critics, who could apply themselves to any material, and not just to those texts, particularly poems, or historical periods, such as the Romantic Era, which pretty well asked for their contradictions to be revealed. The deconstructive methods of philosophy were easily adapted to the paradox-hunting, metaphor-undoing techniques of literary theory, to which they gave an often spurious and portentous significance. In the work of de Man, Hillis Miller, and other Yale-situated disciples of Derrida, a great deal of enlivening attention was paid to the self-defeating *rhetoric of argument* in literary works and elsewhere, particularly by an analysis of their hidden metaphors, of the kind exemplified above. Works of art were seen as inexorably disabled by the contradictory implications of the figurative, and so – and this is the point – they were cut off from any reliable relationship to history, and from any sustained claims as to matters of empirical fact. In this way, the philosophy behind deconstruction inspired a huge expansion of interest in literary theory, whose concerns came to dominate whole schools of literary criticism.

The best protection against this kind of critique, and the best way of signalling that one was up to date enough to be aware of it, whether in doing philosophy, making theory, or creating art, was to become very self-conscious indeed concerning one's own position, and to build in the appropriate qualifications about it. This self-conscious *reflexivity*, whose symptom was a frequent recourse to metalanguages, was seen by some as the hallmark of philosophy under postmodern conditions. In a great amount of postmodernist work, then, a reflexive self-critique or regress is literally written into the 'text'. This can be seen in Godard's films, which are, according to the Marxist theorist Frederic Jameson,

> resolutely postmodernist in that they conceive of themselves as sheer text, as a process of production of representations that have no truth content, are, in this sense, sheer surface or superficiality. It is this conviction which accounts for the reflexivity of the Godard film, its resolution to use representation against itself to destroy the binding or absolute status of any representation.
>
> Frederic Jameson, cited in Hans Bertens, *The Idea of the Postmodern* (1994)

This postmodernist awareness of the *work as text*, even if it is a film or a painting or a fashion show, sees any significant cultural product as continuous with all other uses of natural language. This avoided any 'aesthetic' privileging of the individual artwork and its unitary organization, which was seen as a typically modernist error. The claim was rather that the work had a continuity with all other texts. Postmodernist deconstruction thus forced another parallel between the discourse of philosophy (a highly technical discipline which returns again and again to the same problems, and roots out contradiction) and that of works of art, and indeed all the discourses of society.

Given the severe restraints that it placed upon the possibility of achieving the unity of coherent argument, and the great suspicion that arose concerning the more or less hidden debt of any work or text to its predecessors, it came to be thought that any text, from philosophy to the newspapers, involved an obsessional repetition or *intertextuality*. Just as much as philosophy, which since Plato has worried away at the same old problems, the novel will inevitably reproduce or re-represent earlier positions, earlier ideas, conventional modes of description, and so on. And not only Joyce's *Ulysses*, that is, a deliberately allusive modernist work, can do this. As Umberto Eco, a significant postmodern theorist, put it in his amazingly popular postmodernist novel *The Name of the Rose*: 'books always speak of other books, and every story tells a story that has already been told'. This view ends up in a kind of textual idealism, because all texts are seen as perpetually referring to other ones, *rather than to any external reality.* No text ever finally establishes anything about the world outside itself. It never comes to rest, but merely, to use Derrida's term, 'disseminates' variations on previously established concepts or ideas.

Rewriting history

As I have already asserted, all this activity kept realism of all kinds in the dock. To attempt any form of realism was to fall into philosophical error, and so the attempt to write history from the hitherto dominant positivist or empiricist point of view was doomed to failure. Once again, postmodernist thought, by analysing everything as text and rhetoric, tended to push hitherto autonomous intellectual disciplines in the direction of literature – history was just another narrative, whose paradigm structures were no better than fictional, and was a slave to its own (often unconsciously used) unrealized myths, metaphors, and stereotypes. Its sources, however objective or evidence-based they might seem to be, were in the end just another inter-related series of multiply interpretable texts, and even its causal explanations could be shown to derive from, and hence to repeat, well-known fictional plots.

This view of the writing of history is an essential test of postmodernist doctrine as it affects all parts of our culture. If even history fails, under postmodernist scrutiny, to come up to the previously dominant 'realist' or 'positivist' criteria for its writing, then literature, which is further removed from history, cannot make any strong realist claims either. The basic postmodernist claim here is that the notion of *objective* reconstruction according to the evidence is just a myth. Historians can't simply tell us how things were, or how they are, because, as Alun Munslow puts it, all 'meaning is generated by socially encoded and constructed discursive practices that mediate reality so much that they effectively close off direct access to it'. History is therefore at base just another more or less socially acceptable narrative, competing for our attention and our assent; just another way of putting things, which will survive, or not, through a process of discussion and debate. What is more, its elaborate causal constructions and explanations are essentially put together in the way that fictional narratives are. As Hayden White writes:

> historical narratives . . . are verbal fictions, the contents of which are as much invented as found and the forms of which have more in common with their counterparts in literature than they have with those in the sciences.
>
> Hayden White, 'The Historical Text as a Literary Artifact' in his *Tropics of Discourse* (1978)

All history books tell you a story, where the most basic evidence or facts, such as that 'Napoleon was short' or that 'Cleopatra's nose was a beautiful one and not a centimetre too long' can give rise to interminable, essentially disputable interpretations, which also make factual claims, for example ' . . . and therefore Napoleon was compensatorily aggressive, and Cleopatra irresistibly attractive'. For these judgements will in their turn fit into larger, typical narratives, in which, for example, Napoleon's conquests are largely to be interpreted as manifestations of his character rather than of underlying economic conditions, or, as Shakespeare seems to have believed following Plutarch, Antony fled from the Battle of Actium because of Cleopatra's amazing erotic appeal. It doesn't matter whether the storyteller here is a great historian or William Shakespeare: they both fix upon a narrative shape or genre for what they have to tell us, which they will borrow from the currently available conventions for making them. Some postmodernist-influenced histories, for example Simon Schama's *Citizens: A Chronicle of the French Revolution* (1989) and Orlando Figes's *A People's Tragedy: The Russian Revolution 1891–1921* (1996), make this narrative function quite clear. We are following a story, but no historian can claim that this one is *the* story, even if that is what he or she is aiming at. Apart from anything else, the relationship between the 'invented' or 'constructed' and the 'found' or the 'evidential' will always be a matter of dispute or interpretation. This is certainly so for the complex cases that are most interesting to us: very simple accounts, which show that the relationship of fact to story can at least in some cases be 'indisputable', won't get us very far with an understanding of the cultural practices of writing history of the kind that counts in the world, such as informs our understanding of the relationship of American historical writing to beliefs about the Cold War, or of the left-wing history of dissent and opposition, or whether the Rosenbergs were guilty, or how Kennedy came to be shot in Texas. And the cultural selectivity (from this point of view) of most historical accounts has been amply demonstrated by feminist historians.

What is more, at the most basic level, the novelist and the historian will be using a language full of tropes or metaphors; these also signify to us the way in which history is far from being concerned with mere literal facts. It isn't just the causal relationships of the historical plot that are at issue here, but all the conventional and not-so-conventional pathways in language that we have inherited.

And from this, according to the postmodernists, other characteristics of history might be expected to flow. Most obviously, if the very possibility of a realist history is denied, if facts are always to be seen as merely relative to the theoretical presuppositions which constitute them, and to the interpretations which are made of them, and if the evidence is always to be seen in relation to the construction of a context for it, even the most dry-as-dust, apparently non-narrative approach to historical evidence or 'primary sources' will inevitably carry narrrative presuppositions. History will have an essentially mythological shape, which reveals itself most clearly in fiction and provides the basic conceptual structure for history. If it is accepted that the use of such essentially interpretative structures is inevitable, then postmodernist relativism is the norm, because these competing, myth-derived structures are clearly in competition. If direct access to the past is denied, all we can have are competing stories, which are variously given coherence by their historian narrators, and the past is no more than what the historians, whom we rely upon for various cultural reasons, try to say that it is. And what is more, for many postmodernists, the narrative structures favoured by historians will carry unavoidable and possibly objectionable philosophical or ideological implications – for example, a far too novelistic and bourgeois belief in the importance of individual human agency in preference to an attribution to underlying economic structures, as in the examples cited above.

But what, then, of our sense of the true, the reliable, the probably true, when we read history? Even consciously postmodernist reconstructionists are trying to help us to form *better* beliefs about what they think actually happened. And there is such a thing as a more or less adequately descriptive narrative. A large amount of correspondence between language and reality is possible. Hardly anyone is in favour of suppressing what is generally accepted as evidence. There is a strong sense in which historians are not free just to make things up, as controversy over the 'Holocaust deniers' has shown. But then realist novelists aren't particularly free to make things up either. They have to know much of what the historian knows, and more. Postmodernist relativism needn't mean that *anything* goes, or that faction and fiction are the same as history. What it does mean is that we should be more sceptically aware, more relativist about, more attentive to, the theoretical assumptions which support the narratives produced by all historians, whether they see themselves as empiricists or deconstructors or as postmodernist 'new historicists'.

This applies as much to postmodernist as to traditional historians. To give an example (reported in Richard Evans's *In Defence of History*, see References), when Diane Purkiss attacks Keith Thomas's account of witches, as being often enough powerless old beggar-women, she says that he is simply repeating an 'enabling myth' in which men's 'historical identity is grounded in the powerlessness and speechlessness of women'. Richard Evans replies to this, in support of Thomas, that 'poor single old women were often accused of witchcraft because, far from being speechless, they cursed those men who refused them alms'. It seems as though Thomas's empirical claims here have simply run foul of Purkiss's rival organizing principle for historical narrative – that it should be used to support contemporary notions of female empowerment.

An exact correspondence between narrative and 'the past' is not possible. We can describe the 'same' event in many different ways, our access to the evidence is always mediated, nothing is simply transparent, and there are always absences and gaps and biases to be dealt with. But narratives can still be more or less adequate to the (interpreted) evidence, and new evidence can still overturn narratives. Moreover, not all literary forms of narrative are equally appropriate to historical periods and events. As Munslow points out, the 1944 Warsaw Ghetto Uprising is not equally appropriately narrated, and therefore well interpreted, if it is seen as romance, as farce, and as tragedy. The best we can have is a debate about the nature and meaning of past events, and postmodernists (and plenty of others) say that this debate should be kept as open and as rigorous as possible. The penalty of a lack of vigilance is that some 'official version' may come to represent for us a true and final account of the past. It may also thus come to form part of an unjustifiable, because clearly distorting, 'dominant ideology' within its receiving society, as seems to have happened to both sides in the period of the Cold War. On this account the deconstructionist historian differs from the others only in a tendency to worry aloud, as he or she writes, about the difficulties of the job.

Attacking science

Postmodernists got into their most radical political positions (and their most obvious difficulties) in attacking the objectivist claims of science. For scientists obviously think of themselves as contributing to the construction of some unifying theory or 'grand récit' for their subject matter, and they think that they are trying to complete a picture of what is really 'out there' (though this formulation also has its obviously misleading metaphorical model behind it). Can we have a 'picture' of a black hole or of an $n + 4$-dimensional space?

The claims of science were to be called into question. And yet who could now seriously deny the 'grand narrative' of evolution, except someone in the grip of a far less plausible master narrative such as Creationism? And who would wish to deny the truth of basic physics? The answer was, 'some postmodernists', on the political grounds, *inter alia*, that the hierarchizing logic of scientific thought is inherently and objectionably subordinating. For example, Bruno Latour's (absurd) contention that Einstein's relativity theory is 'a contribution to the sociology of delegation' since it involves the writer, Einstein, of the scientific paper imagining the sending out of observers, to make timed measurements of events, which are then shown by the theory to be relative to one another; for Latour, it seems, social concepts can explain basic science.

Most of us think of scientists as those who really know how things are: they reveal the nature of nature; their knowledge of causal laws enables us to produce inventions that make a difference, like microchips; their standards of evidence, of verification and general consensus, which ultimately control the paradigms or conceptual frameworks within which they work, are (or should be) the best we know (far better, for example, than those current amongst economists). That is what a Nobel Prize means.

But postmodernists do not like this picture. They have attacked the basic claims traditionally made by scientists:

(1) that they can describe and analyse, objectively and truthfully, and therefore with a universal application, the physical reality which surrounds us, and

(2) that their scientific inquiry is a disinterested pursuit of truths about reality, which are also universalizable, in that they are true everywhere, quite independent of any merely local cultural constraints, and in particular independent of any of the more or less hidden moral or ideological motivations which may have inspired their discovery.

For postmodernists, who are good relativists, scientists can have no such privileges: they promote just 'one story among many', their pretensions are unjustified. They do not so much 'discover' the nature of reality as 'construct' it, and so their work is open to all the hidden biases and metaphors which we have seen postmodernist analysis reveal in philosophy and ordinary language. The key questions about science should not therefore just centre on its inflated (logocentric) claims to truth, but on the political questions aroused by its institutional status and application, shaped as they are by the ideological agendas of powerful elites. This is an extreme version of the relativism we have already encountered, for the attack on science is not just about philosophical constructions of the world, which have always been in dispute, but about those empirically based analyses of the world (in medicine and computer development, as much as in aeronautics and bomb manufacture) that seem to have been most successfully 'true'.

In considering this postmodernist attack, we need, in the interests of clarity, to keep the epistemological and the ideological issues as separate as possible. It is, of course, the point that deconstructive postmodernists and their followers wish to make, that these two claims are not, from their point of view, separable at all. But I refuse simply to assume that they are right. For it is surely perfectly obvious, and nothing new, that the *motivations* for and consequences of scientific discovery are open to moral and political criticism. Many of those who worked on the atom bomb, notably Robert Oppenheimer, were acutely aware of that. Quantum mechanics, genetic engineering, and our scientific knowledge of the global climate of course have interestingly different relationships to the financing and pursuit of Western political and military objectives. But these contextual judgements can be accepted without it following that the core activities of scientists are somehow unsuccessful in arriving at the most reliable way of analysing nature we can manage. There is something very odd indeed in the belief that in looking, say, for causal laws or a unified theory, or in asking whether atoms really do obey the laws of quantum mechanics, the activities of scientists are somehow *inherently* 'bourgeois' or 'Eurocentric' or 'masculinist', or even 'militarist'.

This is, partly at least, because the truths of science, rather than those of politics or religion, seem as a matter of fact to be equally valid for socialist, African, feminist, and pacifist scientists (though some persons in these categories deny this). For empirical scientists only accept truths that have this universalizable character. Aspirin works everywhere. It is one of the things that they are not willing to be (politically or culturally) relativist about. Although every scientist can think of cases in which political pressure has led to bad science (as in the official Soviet view of plant genetics, Lysenkoism) and, hopefully, to good science (as in the investigation of AIDS), the results of such investigations will only stand in the long run within the community of scientists if they meet the usual tests, which are independent of any political context.

As two professors of physics, Alan Sokal and Jean Bricmont, have devastatingly pointed out, postmodernist critics of science often grossly fail to understand the empirical claims of science and the ways in which its key theoretical terms work, and often subsitute for them, when they apply scientific modes of thought to the political world, a number of tendentiously vague and misleading metaphors. The result is, as Sokal and Bricmont put it, 'mystification, deliberately obscure language, confused thinking, and the misuse of scientific concepts'. For example, Jean Baudrillard claims that in the Gulf War 'the space of the event has become a hyperspace with multiple refractivity *and the space of war has become definitively non-Euclidean*'. Sokal and Bricmont comment on this that the concept of 'hyperspace' offered here simply 'does not exist in either mathematics or physics' and that it makes no sense to ask what a Euclidean space of war would be like, let alone to hypothesize the kind of space which Baudrillard has just 'invented' through his misunderstanding and misuse of scientific terminology.

And so one reply from scientists to postmodernists is that the latter may have an entirely worthy interest in the sociology and politics of science, but simply don't understand its actual workings, and the nature of the truths it attempts to establish, very well. This riposte parallels the reproach, from philosophers in the Anglo-American tradition, that postmodernists don't understand the workings and successes of logocentric philosophy very well either, and that this may be because the most prestigious postmodernist theorists don't seem to be very interested in constructive dialogue with anyone but each other. Their eagerness to embrace what seem to be 'politically correct' positions has too often led them to express utterly bizarre and ill-informed, not to say politically biased, accounts of what scientists are doing. This is the main burden of the publications of Sokal and others (notably after Sokal in 1994 had a hoax account of scientific activity, full of elementary scientific howlers and non sequiturs, published by a postmodernist journal, *Social Text*).

For many postmodernist attacks on science, which attempt to demonstrate the inherently political characteristics of empiricist Western scientific activity, are not just ill-informed but peculiarly Pickwickian, in that they tend to do little more than import metaphors or analogies into the findings of science, to the point that under the kind of deconstructive analysis described above they look as though they imply some kind of political statement or position that is in fact quite irrelevant to the truths they are trying to establish.

For example, there is a much referred to article by the anthropologist Emily Martin on 'The Egg and the Sperm', which argues that 'the picture of egg and sperm drawn in popular as well as scientific accounts of reproductive biology relies on stereotypes central to our cultural definitions of male and female'. 'The stereotypes imply not only that female biological processes are less worthy than their male counterparts but also that women are less worthy than men'. In such literature, it is asserted, we have a 'passive', 'coy damsel' female egg, versus the 'active', 'macho' male sperm, and it does indeed seem that some textbook accounts do employ this tendentious imagery. But there is more to it than this. Patriarchal scientists are supposed by their postmodernist critics to have inevitably, given their subjective and politically contaminated presuppositions, got the science of this relationship wrong. For it is now believed that the (female) egg actively 'grabs the (male) sperm' (which has swum a long way before this happens). But did male ideological presuppositions about male superiority and aggression as a matter of fact hold up or block the new view? Does it make sense, as an account of scientific activity, to say that any such presuppositions could have produced this particular hold up? (This is not to deny that male preoccupations have indeed held up the proper investigation of female physiology.)

There are two issues here. One is the metaphorical resonance that various accounts of the egg and sperm have in relationship to gender stereotypes – for example, Scott Gilbert builds on this to write (vulgarly) about 'fertilisation as a kind of martial gang-rape' – 'the egg is a whore attracting the soldiers like a magnet', and so on. But this resonance is in any case a gross exaggeration: no such phrases actually appear in the serious scientific literature on this subject. All of this metaphorical interpretation, typical though it is of postmodernist concerns, seems to me relatively trivial and silly, and doesn't have far to go, because anyone who wanted to generalize either view of sperm and egg relations to justify or explain the nature of any larger-scale male–female interactions would surely be expressing a ludicrous essentialism – 'it's been like that from the sperm and egg on'. This sort of thing rather misses the point about the potential for adjustment in male–female relations; but it also makes a much more damaging second implication about science – that there was a failure of objectivity here, and that the 'new' discovery corrected a masculinist bias in scientific work. But, as Paul Gross shows, it is quite false to claim that male scientists had ignored the active role of the female egg until prodded into admitting it by feminists. It had been pointed out by Just in 1919 (also citing a paper of 1878) that the egg 'pulls in' or 'engulfs' the sperm. And this view was common, says Gross, in textbooks from 1920 onwards.

All these radical postmodernist arguments are now under severe attack, but they have very much changed the way in which the scientific disciplines are perceived within American and European culture, towards a more sceptical, and politicized, view.

Of course, it hardly needs to be added that 'realist' history and novel writing, film making, science, and newspaper reporting also continued on their way in the era of postmodernist theory; they had a high level of general acceptability, so that many of those attracted to postmodernist art and theory must have found themselves living in two opposing epistemological worlds.

This battle between postmodernists and others in philosophy and theory and history and science was basically about the claims of unificatory versus contradictionist talk, the contrast between cooperative constructing and individualist deconstructing. But each side needs the other. Postmodernists liberally opposed all holistic explanations (even if they sometimes readmitted them through the back door by promoting arguments which were in sympathy with those of Freud and Marx), and their oppositional, negative postmodernist critique was, as we shall see, in many ways immensely liberating, certainly for women, for cultural minorities, and for much of the artistic avant-garde. An artist's ideas can perhaps more truly be seen as 'play' than those of a historian or scientist, or indeed of a lawyer, who could hardly apply a postmodernist scepticism to the law of evidence or to the notion that one way or another the courts are designed to test the truth or probability of two alternative accounts of what actually happened.

Postmodernist critical techniques were much more successfully applied to ethical and social problems, for example to the 'undoing' of the 'grand recit' of patriarchy and the defence of women against its dominance. I turn now to these ethical and political concerns.

Chapter 3
Politics and identity

Yes, I could have been a judge but I never had the Latin, never had the Latin for the judging, I just never had sufficient of it to get through the rigorous judging exam. They're noted for their rigour. People come staggering out saying, 'My God, what a rigorous exam' – and so I became a miner.

Peter Cook, *Beyond the Fringe* (1961)

The most important postmodernist ethical argument concerns the relationship between discourse and power. A 'discourse' here means a historically evolved set of interlocking and mutually supporting statements, which are used to define and describe a subject matter. Crudely, it's the language of the main intellectual disciplines, for example the 'discursive practices' of law, medicine, aesthetic judgement, and so on. These discourses, as used by lawyers, doctors, and others, do not just implicitly accept some kind of dominating theory to guide them (for example, in the guise of a paradigm as used by those engaged in orthodox science). They involve politically contentious activities, not just because of the certainty with which they describe and define people – who is an 'immigrant', or an 'asylum seeker', or a 'criminal', or 'mad', or a 'terrorist' – but because such discourses at the same time express the political *authority* of their users.

Prisoner: As God is my judge, my Lord, I am not guilty.
Judge: He is not. I am. You are. Six months.

The power of words

All reasonably systematic uses of language are to be seen as having a particular power-enforcing function. You believe what the young surgeon tells you, and so give him permission to anaesthetize you, cut you up, and help you recover. The language game of the discourse expresses and enacts the authority of those who are empowered to use it within a social group, which includes hospitals, law courts, boards of examiners, and professors like me writing books like this. It can also be used to subordinate or exclude or marginalize those who are outside it – witches, mesmerists, faith healers, homosexuals, Communist sympathizers, anarchist protesters. Here is one of the many connections with the philosophical themes explored above.

The most influential analysis of this relationship between discourse and power was given by Michel Foucault in his studies of the history of practices in law, penology, and medicine. Such powerful discourses are rather obviously designed to exclude and control people, such as those diagnosed as criminally insane or ill. And these exclusions arise for Foucault in a classically Marxist manner:

> The general juridical form that guaranteed a system of rights that were egalitarian in principle was unsupported by these fine, everyday, physical mechanisms, by all those systems of micro-power that are essentially non-egalitarian and asymmetrical that we call the 'disciplines' such as exams, hospitals, prisons, the regulation of workshops, schools, the army.
>
> Michel Foucault, *Discipline and Punish: The Birth of the Prison* (1977)

Foucault adopts the victim's position, and analyses power from the bottom up, and not simply as an imposition of the interests of the class above. He tries to show that the will to exercise power beats humanitarian egalitarianism every time, and implies that even the

Enlightenment reliance upon universal principle and reason is always incipiently totalitarian, because the appeal to an always-correct Reason is itself a system of control and will always exclude what it makes marginal, simply by seeing it as non-rational. For Foucault, these supposed irrationalities would include matters of desire, feeling, sexuality, feminity, and art.

Foucault is deeply anti-progressive – he is an anti-Whig historian who chronicles the rise of unfreedom. In doing this, he looks for what he calls the 'episteme', that is, the largely unconscious assumptions concerning intellectual order that underlie the historical states of particular societies. These are the 'historical *a priori*' conditions of a period, which 'delimit the totality of experience in a field of knowledge', define the mode of being of the objects in the field, and 'provide man's everyday perceptions with theoretical powers'. They also define the conditions under which a discourse can be 'true'. We need to dig for this in history, hence what Foucault calls the 'archaeology' of the episteme. These conditions lie below perception, they are not always explicit, so that the episteme is a kind of epistemological unconscious for an age.

Foucault subjects all this material to a leftist critique to show what and whom it excludes, and how. Power and knowledge fundamentally interact, for example when the medically trained 'reasonable' people define themselves against the 'unreasonable' and, having made their judgement, proceed to lock them up in asylums. Sexists, racists, and imperialists all use similar techniques – they make *their* 'normalizing' discourse prevail, and, in doing so, they can actually create or bring into being the deviant or what many postmodernists call *the other*. Their discourse actually helps to *create* the subordinate identities of those who are excluded from participation in it.

Foucault takes homosexuals, women, the criminally insane, non-whites, and prisoners as standard examples of the 'other'. This opposition and antipathy is really quite obvious in schools, armies, and in the process of imperial rule, and so postmodernist thought has inspired much work on the nature of the 'postcolonial subject'. What is distinctive here of postmodernism is the basis of the analysis in the linguistic – as we have already seen in looking at Derrida and Barthes. People become signs, part of the play of language – hence, for example, Laura Mulvey's much-cited and frequently reprinted 'Visual Pleasure and Narrative Cinema', which includes the magnificently overconfident generalization that

> Woman, then stands in patriarchal culture as a signifier for the male other, bound by a symbolic order in which man can live out his fantasies and obsessions through linguistic command by imposing them on the silent image of a woman still tied to her place as a bearer of meaning, not maker of meaning.
>
> *Screen* 16, no. 3, Autumn 1975

We thus talk people into being (just as we do universities and the Euro). But the postmodernists go on from this to make an important, more general point. 'Discourse', from this point of view, is like a Derridean language – it isn't the property of controlling individuals; it goes beyond them. Nor is it only to be found in obviously formal contexts, like that of the law court. It is out and about in society from top to bottom, from the pronouncements of judges to scientific journals to TV advertisement, pop songs, and the broadsheets of the day. And the more dominant a discourse is within a group or society, the more 'natural' it can seem, and the more it tends to appeal to the ways of nature to justify itself. 'Nature' as a whole may seem to proclaim the ordering powers of a god, or the hidden order discovered by scientists; or to contain 'breeds beyond the pale', or women, or the mad, who are to be thought of as *inherently*, that is naturally, more animal, less reasonable, than 'us', and so on. We internalize these subordinating norms, which, as Derrida and Foucault point out, are often intimately part of our language, without always realizing that this is what they are: we go along with them unwittingly, as if they were facts about nature

47

rather than psychologically and politically motivated features of our talk about it.

The asylum, for example, as described by Foucault, is driven by the discourses of the doctor, and mirrors the authoritarian structures of the bourgeois society which surrounds it. It is a microcosm for family, transgression, and madness relations. Foucault, on the other hand (or rather, on the left), is in favour of 'folly', and against bourgeois reason, and although his history of asylums is not nearly as empirically well founded as it ought to be, the political point he wished to make about authority and power went home. Like so many in the 1960s (such as the analyst R. D. Laing in his *The Divided Self*, or Ken Kesey in his novel *One Flew Over the Cuckoo's Nest*), Foucault casts the insane in the role of society's victims, and stresses society's failure to see that the insane are also deeply unhappy individuals. He makes a similar analysis (and a similar overgeneralization) about prisons, which supposedly reveal the basic 'carceral' nature of the society around them. Society, in Foucault's Kafkaesque rewrite of Orwell's *1984*, suffers from a 'universal panopticism'. We are all being secretly surveyed and controlled. But this is to pretend that the usual forms of social control, like working to a routine and being supervised, are the same thing as being in prison. But 'society' and 'prison' are not the same.

I have given above some obvious examples of the abuse of power. These offend our Enlightenment intuitions about universal justice and the right of the individual to autonomy. But it is one of Foucault's many defects that he fails to give anything like an *ethical* account of power in general. He wants 'struggle' rather than submission, but he doesn't very clearly say why. For him, 'power' seems to be a kind of electrical force, an inevitable accompaniment to all human activity, like gravity. Although his thought presupposes a leftist, indeed Marxist, analysis, he avoids any obvious political commentaries and moral theories, and so in the end, although he is a classical 'resister', he does little more than recommend, rather as Lyotard does, small-scale, local reforms. As Terry Eagleton puts it:

> Foucault objects to particular regimes of power not on moral grounds . . . but simply on the grounds that they are regimes as such, and so, from some vague libertarian standpoint, repressive.
>
> Terry Eagleton, *The Illusions of Postmodernism* (1996)

Just as importantly, in looking at the functions of discourse, Foucault fails to allow for the ways in which it actually works through individuals, and so he underestimates the importance of individual agency and responsibility. We all know we should distrust Angelo in Shakespeare's *Measure for Measure* when he says to Isabella, 'It is the law not I, condemns your brother'. For Foucauldians, it is not so much the individual who does dreadful things as the discourse of power that flows through him or her. Foucault thus provides a sophisticated, language-based version of the class antagonisms of Marx – he relies on beliefs about the inherent evil of the individual's class position, or professional position, seen as 'discourse', regardless of the morality of his or her individual conduct.

Readers of this book will have hardly failed to notice the unwillingness of politicians to accept individual responsibility for their actions, or even for that of their subordinates, as they used to do. They also tend to express wildly prejudiced views, on the grounds that they are held by 'large numbers of people', perhaps recent immigrants or those seeking asylum, or neighbours of a different ethnic group, and in doing so say that they are merely to be seen as articulating those views as of political importance. In all such cases they just allow discourse to wash through them. And when their conduct has been questionable, they do not simply say 'I did not do it' or 'I did do it', but rather claim to have been exonerated or excused by the discourse of the report that has been made upon their actions. To that extent, they indeed demonstrate the Foucauldian episteme of their age, and with that the disadvantages of an inherently politicizing rather than a moral view of individual responsibility.

Self and identity

The analysis of the relation between discourse and power had a further and important consequence for postmodernists. It led to a distinctive view of the *nature of the self* which was a challenge to the individualist rationalism, and the emphasis on personal autonomy, of most liberals. Indeed, the term preferred by postmodernists to apply to individuals is not so much 'self' as 'subject', because the latter term implicitly draws attention to the 'subject-ed' condition of persons who are, whether they know it or not, 'controlled' (if you are on the left) or 'constituted' (if you are in the middle) by the ideologically motivated discourses of power which predominate in the society they inhabit.

The extraordinary achievement of Foucault and those who thought like him was, given their analysis of the workings of power, to go on to make one of the most influential of postmodernist claims – the claim that such discourses entailed, imposed, demanded (the many possibilities here constitute the interest of the claim) a particular kind of *identity* for all those who were affected by them. In postmodernist jargon, they '*constitute the subject*'. Of course, the fact that institutions and their discourses demand that you be a particular sort of person, to 'fit in', was hardly unknown. Anyone who has been in a school or sports team or military organization or given birth to a baby in a hospital, let alone read some of the 'Organization Man' sociology of the 1950s, is to some degree aware of this point. But the postmodernist argument was an exceptionally subtle one. We don't just *play roles* in such cases, but our very identity, the notion we have of ourselves, is at issue when we are affected by discourses of power. These, of course, run from those which are directly concerned with matters of identity (in religion, and in therapy from Freudianism to psycho-babble), to those which are far less obviously so, as in the case of a woman responding to the female lead in a male-dominated Hollywood film, or to paintings of the nude in the male-dominated museum, or the teenager in front of the TV set. All discourses put you in your place. (I am as usual citing examples that are more everyday and intuitively appealing than the rather heavily buried and theorized examples to be found in the abounding academic literature of postmodernism.)

Postmodernist critics go on to make political claims concerning the nature of the 'subject'. One of these is that the conflicting languages of power which circulate through and within individuals actually constitute the self. The subject cannot on this view ever 'stand aside' from actual social conditions and judge them from a rational, autonomous point of view, as moral philosophers in the Anglo-American Kantian tradition, like John Rawls and Thomas Nagel, argue. The thoughts and expressions of the male individual, for example, are seen as part of a pattern of contaminated, patriarchal discourses, which are in any case in conflict, and of which he is the mere epiphenomenon. This chucks out the Kantian, unifying ego in favour of a postmodernist updating of the Freudian model, of persons as undergoing an internal conflict between systems. As Seyla Benhabib, a Professor of Government at Harvard University, puts it (conflating as she does so Derridean and Foucauldian language about language):

> The subject is replaced by a system of structures, oppositions and differances which, to be intelligible, need not be viewed as products of a living subjectivity at all. You and I are the mere 'sites' of such conflicting languages of power, and 'the self' is merely another position in language.
>
> Seyla Benhabib, *Situating the Self* (1992)

The consequences of this view of the nature of the individual can be very clearly seen in many postmodernist literary texts, which contrast in this respect with the liberal tradition of the novel as continued in this period by writers like Angus Wilson, Iris

Murdoch, John Updike, Philip Roth, and Saul Bellow. For a literary critic and historian of postmodernism like Linda Hutcheon, such novels as Salman Rushdie's *Midnight's Children* challenge 'the humanist assumption of a unified self and an integrated consciousness'. Postmodernist fiction

> puts into question that entire series of interconnected concepts that have come to be associated with what we conveniently label as liberal humanism: autonomy, transcendence, certainty, authority, unity, totalisation, system, universalisation, centre, continuity, teleology, closure, hierarchy, homogeneity, uniqueness, origin.
>
> Linda Hutcheon, *A Poetics of Postmodernism* (1988)

And so, in much recent American fiction

> The focus of attention has shifted from the psychology of character (an irreducible essence, something 'human') to the inadequacy of the concept of character, to a recognition of subjectivity as the trace of plural and intersecting discourses, of non-unified, contradictory ideologies, the product of a relational system which is finally that of discourse itself.
>
> Peter Currie, 'Eccentric Selves' in Malcolm Bradbury and
> D. J. Palmer (eds), *Contemporary American Fiction* (1987)

A classic and influential instance is the title story of John Barth's *Lost in the Funhouse* (1968) in which the narrator, Ambrose, describes the difficulty of writing a story called 'Lost in the Funhouse' about a character called Ambrose who is lost in the funhouse. He is supposed to be visiting Ocean City with his family, some time during the last war, part of which involves going to a funhouse. But he is described by an author who is perpetually aware of the fact that he is *telling a story*, and that he is using literary conventions to do so. 'So far,' he says, 'there's been no real dialogue, very little sensory detail, and nothing in the way of a *theme*.' And Ambrose is just a function of his author's story, so that 'One possible ending would be to have Ambrose come across another lost person in the dark'. We are perpetually deprived of any illusion of Ambrose's autonomy, in favour of our seeing him (truthfully enough) as the creature of the person who is writing him, who also acts like a stereotypical Author, who (as his remarks about the function of italics, or the lack of a climax in his own story, imply) seems to be trying to apply the correct rules for narrative which he has learned in writing school.

What goes for a character in a novel goes for authors: they too are spoken by the language they give speech to. (That of the writing school, for example.) And it goes too for the reader, who is in no better case than the author, also being 'dispersed among the interstices of language, enmeshed with and finally lost among the endless relay of signification'. A 'human being' on this view is

> not a unity, not autonomous, but a process, [is] perpetually in construction, perpetually contradictory, perpetually open to change.
> Catherine Belsey, *Critical Practice* (1980)

The postmodernist notion of human identity as essentially constructed like a fiction is also to be found in the visual arts, as is to be seen in Cindy Sherman's series of photographs, *Untitled Film Stills* (1977–80) and its successors. In each of these Sherman impersonates film actresses, disguising herself more or less in different clothing and in different implied situations, which are typical or stereotypical in film. In the process we see her adapting the discourses of film to present herself in a photographic still as all sorts of different people, but all (often satirical or parodic) versions of femininity are seen in the discourses of a mass medium. Of course, this is just another version of acting, but the photographs are not based on any particular film, and they rather schematically raise questions about the ways in which Sherman can preserve or not preserve an underlying identity in all these different roles. In so doing they also put into question the notion of the 'real' Cindy Sherman. Which photographs could possibly convince us that we are seeing this? An open, sincere, emotional, or even naked one?

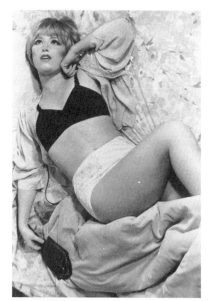

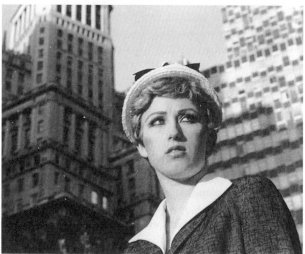

3, 4. Untitled film still (1977) by Cindy Sherman.
Cindy Sherman as Hitchcock or as Antonioni might have seen her;
but didn't.

But each of these would be just the result of another convention, another discourse.

For Roland Barthes the ideal postmodernist work of art recognizes these strategies and playful limitations on human identity and discourse, precisely because this play and division has desirable moral consequences. It disposes of precisely that Kantian unity of the person which makes for social order and moral orthodoxy.

> The pleasure of the text does not prefer one ideology to another. *However* this impertinence does not proceed from liberalism but from perversion: the text, its reading, are split. What is overcome, split, is the moral unity that society demands of every human product.
>
> Roland Barthes, *The Pleasure of the Text* (1975)

Barthes exemplifies his own remarkably evasive doctrine in his 'autobiographical' works, notably through the novelistic conception of himself in *A Lover's Discourse* (1977) in which the grammar of French in the original adroitly keeps the sexual orientation of the protagonist ambiguous (as does the language of Auden's love poetry). And *Roland Barthes by Roland Barthes* (1975), an autobiography, begins by announcing in an epigraph that 'All of this must be thought of as being said by a character in a novel' ['Tout ceci doit être consideré comme dit par un personnage de roman']. So there are two voices in the book, Barthes's 'own' (or that of the author) which we might infer, and that of Barthes as a fictional character. Barthes also reviewed his own book: this time with a reviewer persona.

Such deconstructions of the moral unity of the subject, and the (classically liberal) desire to help the self to evade some of the repressive ideological boundaries it encounters, are very different things. Indeed, the justification for our desire to evade or redraw such boundaries (such as those which confer sexual identity) *already* depends on a notion of the new moral unity or integrity or autonomy we can achieve, once the restrictive boundary is removed. This becomes obvious when, for example, we are urged to recognize the different but non-fractured identities of the homosexual and the heterosexual (or of male and female) by refusing to fall into the ideological trap analysed by Derrida of seeing the one as an inferior version of the other. What postmodern theory helps us to see is that we are all constituted in a broad range of subject positions, through which we move with more or less ease, so that all of us are combinations of class, race, ethnic, regional, generational, sexual, and gender positions.

Many postmodernists make this rather pessimistic analysis in the hope of liberating us from it. Once we have been made aware of the dire effects of contradictory discourses upon us, we are expected to be able to find some kind of way out.

The politics of difference

Postmodernists may not give a particularly convincing account of the nature of the self as it might appear in a moral philosophy concerned with responsibility, but they do very successfully adapt Foucauldian arguments to show the ways in which discourses of power are used in all societies to *marginalize subordinate groups*. For such discourses of power do not just contribute to the decentring and deconstruction of the self; they also serve to marginalize those people who do not partake in them. Again, there are plenty of these eccentric marginalized figures to be encountered within postmodernist fiction, such as Coalhouse Walker in Doctorow's *Ragtime*, Fevvers in Angela Carter's *Nights at the Circus*, and Saleem Sinai in Rushdie's *Midnight's Children*. Saleem is not of any great social importance, and yet his crisis of identity (along with his magical telepathic relationship to those who were also born at the moment of India's independence) is metaphorically seen as parallel to the crisis of the nation as a whole. He indeed tells us: 'I was linked to history both literally and metaphorically, both actively and passively.' But the political history of India is deconstructed to show that the marginal can be seen as the central, indeed Sinai is diffused (like the reader following his text) into all sorts of surrounding fragmentary narratives. The novel does not try to make any sense of the emotional logic of an individual's life (as is typical of realist fiction) but uses its magic realist techniques to show the self as constituted by the conflicts and contradictions of the historical event, to the point of an absurdist hyperbole, as when Saleem remarks 'Nehru's death . . . too, was all my fault'. Even his face is 'the whole map of India', but by the end of the novel, he is no more than a 'big headed top-heavy dwarf.' (The novel owes a great deal to Gunter Grass's *The Tin Drum*.)

Postmodernist thought, in attacking the idea of a notional centre or dominant ideology, facilitated the promotion of a politics of difference. Under postmodern conditions, the ordered class politics preferred by socialists has given way to a far more diffuse and pluralistic *identity politics*, which often involves the self-conscious assertion of a marginalized identity against the dominant discourse.

An example of this, which is undoubtedly central to the politics of the period since the late 1960s, is the relationship between postmodernism and feminism. The argument here is that women are excluded from the patriarchal symbolic order, or from the dominant male discourse, and indeed that they have been defined or 'othered' as inferior with respect to it. They are subjected to a Derridean 'false hierarchy' by being assigned weak values, opposite to the strong ones invested in masculinity. We saw a bit of this in looking at the egg and sperm controversy.

Much feminist thought therefore has in common with postmodernism that it attacks the legitimating metadiscourse used by males, designed to keep them in power, and it seeks an individual empowerment against this. But I agree with critics of this position, like Benhabib, that the woman who does this shouldn't be seen as occupying 'merely another position in language'. For the postmodernist view of this 'socially constructed' self ignores the way the self is constituted by an individual's maintenance of an original, often idiosyncratic *narrative of him or herself*. This is the key to creativity in the individual. This evidence for the growth of an individual through the socialization process is neglected by 'social construction' theorists of the self. We can, of course, discern the conventional codes, and the allegiances to socially constructed kinds of discourse in anyone's autobiography – but with respect to our own, we are (like Roland Barthes) author and character at once. That is how, although we are made up of heteronomous codes, we can still strive for an autonomy of a classically liberal kind. This sense of autonomy is particularly needed by women, says Benhabib, whose conclusion is that the strong constructivist positions derived from Derrida and Foucault would actually 'undermine . . . the theoretical articulation of the emancipatory aspirations of women.' In undermining women's sense of their own agency and sense of selfhood, they deny any reappropriation of women's own history, and the possibility of a radical social criticism. But then the incompatibility of postmodernist attitudes to a commitment to any settled philosophical position (which a good Derridean would then deconstruct) is a grave problem for them. It may indeed be better to follow a rationalist (Enlightenment) egalitarian project of progressive emancipation, as opposed to a postmodernist route, which so often ends up in a radical separatism. For although postmodernist arguments have helped many to *define* the roots of their difference from the majority, or 'those in power', effective political action needs something more than this rather preliminary sense of a dissentient identity.

The liberal would join with the postmodernist in seeing the need for an ability to question the *boundaries* of our social roles, and the validity and dominance of the conceptual frameworks they presuppose; and the postmodernist deconstructive attitude has been extraordinarily effective in combating restrictive ideologies in this way. They often attempt a transgressive-deconstructive loosening of the conceptual boundaries of our thoughts about gender, race, sexual orientation, and ethnicity, and make an essentially liberal demand for the recognition of difference, an acceptance of the 'other' within the community. In such a pluralistic universe (of discourse) no one framework is likely to gain assent. Where epistemological domination is deemed to be impossible, the competition between these conceptual frameworks becomes a political matter, part of a contest for power.

The *postmodernist self*, then, is very differently conceived from the self at the centre of liberal humanist thought, which is supposed to be capable of being autonomous, rational, and centred, and somehow free of any *particular* cultural, ethnic, or gendered characteristics. Postmodernist analysis has turned away from such optimistically universalizable Kantian assumptions to see the self as constituted by language systems, which, although they may most obviously dominate the proletarian, the female, the black, and the colonized, have us all, more or less, in their grip. This general move from a liberal emphasis on self-determination to a Marx-inspired emphasis on other-determination is of immense importance. It is a sharp challenge to established post-Enlightenment, Anglo-American philosophical views, and it points to the irreconcilable differences of identity between individuals. As Robert Hughes has put it in his *The Culture of Complaint*, and admittedly very polemically, it has created a culture in which many were encouraged to see themselves as *victims*. We will look more closely at this culture in the next section.

The result is that although much postmodernist thinking and writing and visual art can be seen as attacking stereotypical categories, defending difference, and so on, it left all these separate groupings to demand recognition as 'authentic' but isolated communities, once they were freed, in and by theory, from the dominant categories of the majority. The beneficiaries of this analysis were both separatist (alienated from and resenting orthodoxy) and partially communitarian (as they identified with others who had similarly defined a dissenting identity). But then how could such differentially defined groups, the result of a categorical freeing up, communicate back with any actually existent political centre? This was difficult, given the sustained and near anarchist hostility of many postmodernists to any overall theory or picture of society.

It is a paradoxical result: a left-inspired distrust of authority (of the Lyotardian kind) makes recognition of difference possible, and yet those who are perhaps most in favour of leaving differently defined groups in isolation, to compete and fight it out, are those on the right, who believe in individual freedom with the minimum amount of state restraint. One of the problems that a critical postmodernism gets itself into, therefore, is that of specifying, independent of grand narratives, or of a 'lapse back' to Kantian or 'essentializing' Enlightenment ideas, the kind of community that would be desirable, once its critique had been made. For the Utopian Marxist, the fact that no such model of community was immediately available didn't much matter; but for thinkers with more short-term, this-worldly aims, it does. The oppositional character of postmodernist thought was therefore maintained, but often at too great a cost. For once all these differences and different identities were established, they were cut off from any central harmonizing ideology. Postmodernists therefore seem to call for an irreducible *pluralism*, cut off from any unifying frameworks of belief that might lead to common political action, and are perpetually suspicious of domination by others. In this, they have turned against those Enlightenment ideals that underlie the legal structures of most Western democratic societies, and that aimed at *universalizable* ideals of equality and justice. Indeed, postmodernists tend to argue that Enlightenment reason, which claimed to extend its moral ideals to all in liberty, equality, and fraternity, was 'really' a system of repressive, Foucauldian control, and that Reason itself, particularly in its alliance with science and technology, is incipiently totalitarian.

This attack on rationality by postmodernists is to some degree comprehensible, in so far as it expressed a Weberian suspicion of the means-end rationalism of technocratic, consumer societies, and of 'capitalist modernization'. But postmodernist scepticism was also directed to the very means of rational communication itself. Jürgen Habermas, one of the most eloquent of leftist critics, is not alone in pointing out that it is very dangerous indeed to take the postmodernist turn, and abandon the ideal of communicative or indeed consensual rationality, which he sees as the best antidote to the political abuse of power. He thinks that we should aim at an 'ideal speech situation'; a means of communication which is so far as is possible undistorted by Foucauldian effects of power, and at just that consensus and sense of social solidarity of which postmodernists are so mistrustful.

For many, the postmodernist position is a disabling one – postmodernists are just epistemological pluralists, with no firm general position available to them, and so, however radical they may seem as critics, they lack a settled external viewpoint, and this means that so far as real-life ongoing politics is concerned, they are passively conservative in effect.

Chapter 4
The culture of postmodernism

The relationship between the climate of ideas outlined in previous chapters and the making of art is a complex one. Not surprisingly, many (but not all) who saw their work as innovatory or avant-garde were attracted to the new critical challenge of postmodernist themes. But it has to be borne in mind that creative people may not need any deep philosophical or academic understanding of such matters. They can also get their 'new ideas' from the conversation and journalism which so often mediate them – and they will sometimes get them wrong, or semi-digested, or exaggerated. But that is the way in which important ideas, like viruses, can catch on in society.

Conversely, postmodernist thinkers and critics have often wished to coopt the artistic avant-garde as exemplars of the importance and influence of their ideas. Lyotard not surprisingly saw it as the job of contemporary artists to question the role of the metanarrative of modernism, which was used to legitimize certain kinds of work. He asks artists to

> question the rules of painting or of narrative as they have learned them from their predecessors. Soon those rules must appear to them as a means to deceive, to seduce, and to reassure, which makes it impossible for them to be 'true'.
>
> Jean-François Lyotard, *The Postmodern Explained to Children: Correspondence 1982–1985* (1992)

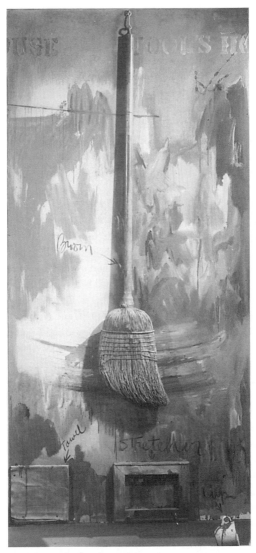

5. *Fool's House* (1962) by Jasper Johns.
Language, theory, the object, and art. Is this a paint brush?

Indeed, it is typical of many postmodernist commentators (such as Andreas Huyssen) that they see the 'true' function of the avant-garde as being critical in the postmodernist sense – it should attack the bourgeois institutions of art and therefore be directed to a (better?) future. Of course, this is far from true of all the avant-garde movements in our period, or before it. It is a political prescription, which would hardly capture, for example, what Charles Jencks and his colleagues (whose view of postmodernism is highly eccentric to that sketched here) would understand by postmodernism, in defending a conservative return to an admittedly parodic neo-Classicist realism in painting and in architecture.

Postmodernist art therefore echoes in very various and often indirect ways the doctrines we have discussed above; it resists the master narrative of modernism, and the authority of high art which modernism itself takes from the past, and it worries about its own language. It is often simply unconcerned by the relationship between the formerly 'high' and 'low' genres, for example as expressed in the two symphonies *Low* (1992) and *Heroes* (1997) by Philip Glass based on the work of David Bowie and Brian Eno, and it can often look quite trivial and popular and tacky. An alliance with popular culture is seen as anti-elitist, anti-hierarchical, and dissenting. It disrupts narrative – as can be seen, for example, in the figurative painting of Eric Fischl and David Salle – because a coherent narrative too easily allies itself to a grand one. (That is why painters like Anselm Kiefer, who devote themselves to grandiose works with a 'deep' relation to history and myth, so significantly lie outside the postmodernist mainstream.) Much postmodernist art pays attention to hitherto marginalized forms of identity and behaviour. This runs from the serious feminist work of Mary Kelly, who documented her relationship to her baby son in *Post Partum Document* (1973–9) ('document' here reveals the nature of the work as a politically significant text, rather than as a formally organized image designed to give visual pleasure) to Madonna's stage performances and her book *Sex* (1992), in which the relationship to

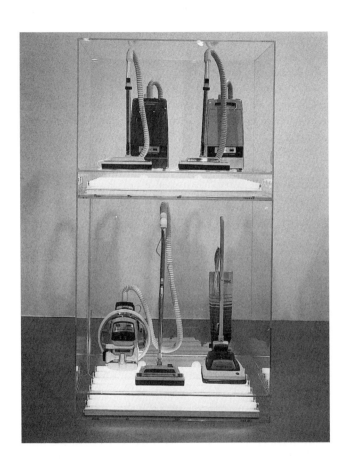

6. *New Hoover Quadraflex* (1981–6) by **Jeff Koons**.
The fine art of museum display is applied to ordinary consumerist objects.

pleasure is entirely different, and which shocked so many feminists for her apparent 'theatrical' submission to sadomasochistic practices, as the 'victim' of men.

This critical attitude, as we shall see, often issues in pastiche, parody, and irony. Hence, for example, Jeff Koons's kitschy *New Hoover Convertible* (1980), which is indeed just a commercially available cleaning machine, floats over fluorescent lights in a plexiglass case. It is a parody of the Duchampian ready-made, because it is indeed a 'desirable' consumerist object (rather than a mere urinal or bicycle wheel). But its economic desirability is loosely confused with, or ironized by, its aesthetic pseudo-admirability, now that it has become a 'work of art' displayed in a museum case rather than packed in a cardboard box to take home. And his *New Hoover Quadraflex* multiplies this by four.

The aim of many working in the avant-garde arts was very often the traditional modernist one, of defamiliarization, now guided by a more radical postmodernist epistemology. The aim, post Derrida, Foucault, and Barthes – whose ideas in variously garbled forms swarm over the pronouncements of artists since the 1970s – was to prevent the consumer-as-subject from feeling 'at home' in the world, for that would lead to a merely conservative pragmatic accommodation to it.

The disruption of any temptation to settle for a familiar world, as opposed to a confrontation with the disturbing qualities of a Barthesian one, is central to the work of Walter Abish, notably in his classically postmodernist narrative *How German Is It?* (1980). Here, both the narrator and the text he creates are subject to radical uncertainties – of plot, causality, theme, and so on – which are mercilessly passed on to the reader, in a tone of wondering scepticism. Consider, for example, the following paragraph from his story 'The English Garden' (out of which *How German Is It?* grew), which is cunningly full of the epistemological traps we have discussed. It runs:

When one is in Germany and one happens not to be German one is confronted with the problem of determining the relevancy and to a certain extent the lifelikeness of everything one encounters. The question one keeps asking oneself is: How German is it? And, is this the true colour of Germany? Looking at the sky one is almost prepared to believe that this is the same sky that the Germans kept watching anxiously in 1923, and 1933 and 1943, that is when they were not distracted by the colour of something else. Something more distracting, perhaps. Now the sky is blue. In German the word is *Blau*. But there are numerous gradations of blue ... numerous choices for every child ... The French say *bleu*, and we say blue.

Walter Abish, *In the Future Perfect* (1977)

It is odd and disconcerting to be asked about the 'lifelikeness' of *everything*. Does one expect an experience of a foreign country as a *whole* to be more like art than life, and hence not lifelike, unreal? Or is it that we don't see it so much as art as through more sinister political and stereotypical preconceptions? The questions Abish asks are so often peculiarly oblique; for example, 'is this the true colour of Germany'? An odd example, for can colours be true? In representations, photographs, and colouring books (all things Abish is much concerned with) they may be true *to* or true *of*, but only when they occur in a copy or reproduction. And of course most paradoxical of all is the fact that colour is one of the things that cannot be conveyed to us by a mere literary text. Our descriptions of it do not suffice.

Abish by this technique makes us realize that we fill in the gaps in the text with our prejudices (or guilts); for example, when he suggests that the Germans may have been 'distracted by the colour of something else'. But what? By grey or brown uniforms? By juxtaposing the 'innocent' 1923 with 1933 and 1943, the text is getting at us, and, as is made clear at the end, the 'us' it is getting at is the English speaker.

Here, and in the brilliant chapter on Gisela and Egon in *How German Is It?*, I think that Abish is finessing upon an argument familiar from Barthes and elsewhere, and trying to trap us into imposing *our* stereotypes upon Gisela and Egon, as representative of what we take to be the 'new Germany'. The text amusingly presents an image (stereotype) by the presentation in language of visual images from a glossy magazine article on Gisela and Egon:

> The meaning, the shades or layers of meaning are to be found in the components: the ubiquitous gabardine suit, the Paisley scarf, the white silk handkerchief displayed in the breast pocket of his jacket, the drooling schnauzer, the black leather trousers, the high-heeled boots, Gisela's swept-back blonde hair, the hairdo emphasizing a sleekness, a sexual sharpness, bringing her pale fine-boned face into greater prominence, the gleaming car with its red leather upholstery and, finally, the partially opened French windows on the ground floor revealing vertical slivers of the interior life. All this to spell out the new German competence and a sense of satisfaction and completion. It is all there . . . the innate German upper- and upper-middle class instinct to combine what is essentially 'perfection' with the 'menacing'.

> Walter Abish, *How German Is It?* (1980)

Postmodernism

Abish thus manoeuvres the reader into a state of sceptical distrust with respect to the text: its humour depends upon the incongruity we feel between the text's dead-pan presentation of the not-quite-stereotypical, and our resistance to it. He produces what Barthes calls a 'text of bliss' –

> a text that imposes a state of loss; a text that discomforts (perhaps to the point of a certain boredom); that unsettles the reader's historical, cultural, and psychological assumptions, the consistency of his or her tastes, values, memories; and brings to a crisis his or her relation with language.

> Roland Barthes, *The Pleasure of the Text* (1975)

The postmodern novel

As the example from Abish is designed to show, the most significant alliance between postmodernist ideas and the artistic culture, in Europe and the United States, has led to a sustained and sceptical relativist critique of the claims of mimesis or realism in the arts. Postmodernist philosophical doubts about the truthfully descriptive relationship of language to the world helped to inspire a kind of art, from the French 'new novel' to magic realist fiction, which relied upon creating all sorts of stimulating confusions between fact and fiction. Brian McHale therefore argues that the 'dominant' mode of postmodernist fiction involves an ontological uncertainty about the contradictory nature of the world projected by the text, and he turns to the work of Beckett, Robbe-Grillet, Fuentes, Nabokov, Coover, and Pynchon in support of his view.

The instability of the fictional 'world' in which we find ourselves, and the difficulty of our coming to know it in any reliable way, is obvious in many such postmodernist fictions. Everything from simple logical contradiction in Robbe-Grillet to paranoia in Pynchon to comic fantasy in Barthelme, to detective stories Chinese-boxed inside other detective stories, as in Paul Auster, gets in the way. In such work, simple facts about the world of the novel are contradicted, there may be no reliable centre of consciousness and the narrator, for example Oedipa Maas in Pynchon's *The Crying of Lot 49* (1967), may be notoriously confused, or perhaps mad, that is, in that ambiguous mental state which affects a fair number of postmodernist protagonists.

An ontological uncertainty is also reinforced by the way in which the *dramatis personae* may wander into the text from history or from other fictions, so that in Coover's *The Public Burning* (1977) President Richard Nixon attempts to seduce Ethel Rosenberg on the eve of her execution, in Doctorow's *Ragtime* (1975) Freud and Jung take a trip together through the Tunnel of Love in an American amusement park, and in Guy Davenport's 'Christ

Preaching at the Henley Regatta' in his *Eclogues* (1981) Bertie Wooster and Mallarmé and Raoul Dufy (who has come to sketch the proceedings and is nearly run down by a Jaguar XKE), and of course Stanley Spencer, stand side by side on the riverbank.

Postmodernist work like this contrasts strongly with modernist fiction, even of the most complex Faulknerian or Joycean kind, which nearly always 'played fair' in the relationship of the text to a (historically) possible world; so that an answer to the puzzle, an intelligible use of cause and effect and a consistent chronology can nearly always be reconstructed by the informed reader. It is just such features that postmodern fiction deconstructs. In staging a confrontation between the world of the text and our own, it enacts a disturbingly sceptical triumph over our sense of reality, and hence also over the accepted narratives of history. The result has been a number of works of art in the distinctively postmodern genre of 'historiographical metafiction'. This mixes historical and fictional material and thereby implies or states a postmodernist critique of the realist norms for the relationship of fiction to history, as we saw Hayden White and others doing earlier.

One of the most popular of those works that play with the notion of history as narrative and with the retrospective ironies that can go with that, is John Fowles's *The French Lieutenant's Woman* (1969), a love story about a Young Darwinian called Charles, his conventional fiancée Ernestina, and a distracting young woman, Sarah Woodruff. The novel not only contains an ironical commentary by the 'author' on the events portrayed (the author knows about Darwin, his hero is only at the beginnings of the discovery of evolution; the author also knows that his heroine is a proto-Existentialist – but she of course does not, as she finally makes her way to a refuge from Fowles's plot in the Chelsea of the Rossettis). There is also a deliberate revealing of the author's manipulations, as he offers a postmodernist commentary on the Victorian period, for example on Victorian attitudes to sex, and on his own plot, which parallels or parodies those of the Victorian novel, particularly Hardy.

This story I am telling is all imagination. These characters I create never existed outside my own mind. If I have pretended until now to know my characters' minds and innermost thoughts, it is because I am writing in (just as I have assumed some of the vocabulary and 'voice' of) a convention universally accepted at the time of my story: that the novelist stands next to God. He may not know all, yet he tries to pretend that he does. But I live in the age of Alain Robbe-Grillet and Roland Barthes; if this is a novel, it cannot be a novel in the modern sense of the word.

So perhaps I am writing a transposed autobiography; perhaps I now live in one of the houses I have brought into the fiction; perhaps Charles is myself disguised. Perhaps it is only a game. Modern women like Sarah exist, and I have never understood them. Or perhaps I am trying to pass off a concealed book of essays on you.

John Fowles, *The French Lieutenant's Woman* (1969)

All this leads to all sorts of serious paradoxes about the characters' thinking of themselves as free, whereas we with hindsight can see them as very much determined by the perspectives (and of course the discourses) of their time. There is as much self-consciousness and reflexivity, relativism, and scepticism here as any postmodernist could want. We can be inside and sympathetic to the characters (typical of the realist novel) at the same time as being outside and judging them (from an ironically inappropriate contemporary point of view). At the end of the novel the 'author', having taken a look at his hero in a railway carriage, offers the reader two alternative endings.

The opening episode of Julian Barnes's *A History of the World in 10½ Chapters* (1989) is an account of Noah's Ark as given by a woodlouse ('anobium domesticum') who is very well informed, it seems, about recent history. For him, the Ark is more like a prison ship; and the bibical account of it is just a myth. This is a parodic, sceptical story about a story, from the bottom level: 'We didn't know anything about the political background. God's wrath with his creation was news to us; we just got caught up in it willy-nilly.' Like so many, one thinks. The technique of the book, as its 10½ stories interact, is perpetually to make us look for such (ironic) parallels to recent political history. (In many of the episodes, socially marginal groups are on a ship and are shipwrecked or attacked.) Not that the woodlouse would have approved of any Official Version – he thinks that *Genesis* discriminates against serpents. His model is a more Darwinian one anyway. God's plan of recruitment for the Ark was entirely incompetent – for example, he forgot to allow for the fact that some animals are a bit slow

> There was a particularly relaxed sloth, for instance – an exquisite creature, I can vouch for it personally – who had scarcely got down to the foot of its tree before it was wiped out in the great wash of God's vengeance. What do you call that – natural selection? I'd call it professional incompetence.

The woodlouse is the worker, the voice of the repressed, criticizing the bosses and their dominant discourse amongst much else in this amazingly inventive book. Noah and his family just eat up odd species on this 'floating cafeteria' (or 'spaceship earth'?). The Ark soon resembles, perhaps, a concentration camp, in which Shem 'had this thing about the purity of the species'. Bible, myth, history, science, and much else all run together in an achronological, ironic, and parodic parallel, in what seems to be an enormous attack on Bible or myth or politics as ideological explanation. The succeeding chapters are equally complex, and they provide an extraordinary compendium of postmodernist attitudes to history, but of course (like Abish) without any of the solemnity of 'theory'.

Works like this

> suggest not only that writing history is a fictional act, ranging events conceptually through language to form a world-model, but that history itself is invested like fiction, with interrelating plots which appear to interact independently of human design.
>
> Patricia Waugh, *Metafiction* (1984)

In such cases, it is the fictional narrative which, in accord with the philosophical scepticism outlined earlier, is allowed to dominate, in the belief that, as we have seen, history is just another narrative, subject to our desires and stereotypical prejudices, and inevitably organized, by Barnes as a woodlouse or Fowles as a Victorian gentleman-author, according to the fictional stereotypes of plot current within the society from which it emanates.

It is not surprising that the novel has borne a disproportionate amount of the burden of being 'postmodern', because its hitherto usual 'discourses' – in the relationship of author to the text, its apparently liberal or 'bourgeois individualist' construction of unified character, its relationship to historical truth – lay it at so many points open to a postmodernist critique. From modernist mastery and formal control, respect for autonomy and individualism, and claims to historical explanatory force, all to be found, for example, when Joyce writes about Dublin or Faulkner about the South, we move towards a playful, disseminatory, self-conscious, evasive, often deliberately falsifying account of characters, who may exist on so many planes at once as to lack all plausible psychological unity. The postmodernist novel doesn't try to create a sustained realist illusion: it displays itself as open to all those illusory tricks of stereotype and narrative manipulation, and of multiple interpretation in all its contradiction and inconsistency, which are central to postmodernist thought. Its internal theorizing, its willingness to display to the reader its own formal workings, is also typically postmodern, not just in the novel, but also in film, for example in Godard's adaptation of the Brechtian technique of the interpolated sign-post or text, and also in visual art, which is so often 'about itself' in this period.

Postmodernist music?

There is not a great deal about music in this book: this is partly because long before the period we are concerned with, many composers had already given up background conventions like those attacked by postmodernism – for example, they had rejected the conventional tonal narrative order of the work. They had also tended to reject the influence of (dominant) past thinkers, who had aimed at the total organization of the piece, from Schoenberg and the twelve-tone method to the totally organized serialism advocated by Boulez and others in the 1960s. These modernist formalisms were no longer of dominating interest. Many composers had indeed earlier been prone to allow theoretical specifications of what was desirable to dictate what they wrote. By the late 1960s many composers abandoned the dream of a theoretically rigorous ordering of sounds and adopted a whole range of strategies which were compatible with the pluralism of postmodernist thought, even if not particularly inspired by it.

There are nevertheless some works that offer pretty close parallels to other postmodernist art, or that were influenced by it. For example, the second movement of Luciano Berio's *Sinfonia* (1968) accepts the metanarrative backbone of the scherzo from Mahler's Second Symphony, which more or less controls its rhythmic movement, but which it then decomposes or deconstructs as it goes along. Along with this, Berio combined a parodic intertextual collage of quotations from all sorts of musical sources – bits of Bach, Schoenberg, Debussy (*La Mer*), Ravel (*La Valse*), and so on – and combines with this a performance of extracts of text from Beckett's *The Unnameable*, slogans from the May 1968 'évènements', quotations from Lévi-Strauss and Martin Luther King, and so on. (He later added a fifth movement to the work which is intended to make a typically self-conscious postmodern meta-commentary on the previous ones.) And one could certainly say that his *Recital – I* (1972) sees the stream of consciousness of its heroic recitalist, which is full of fragments of her repertoire, as showing that her subjectivity is partially socially constructed or 'constituted' by the musical texts that run through her mind.

This intertextual eclectic collage of quotation, which is reminiscent, in its lack of logical connexion, of much postmodernist painting (like that of Salle or Schnabel) is also to be found in the work of Alfred Schnittke, Toru Takemitsu (for example, in his Debussyan *Quotations of Dream*), and many others. The polystylistic collage techniques of Schnittke make an indifferent use of 'high' and 'low' sources, so that his *Concerto Grosso I* (1977) includes, as described in the preface to the score, 'formulae and forms of Baroque music; free chromaticism and micro-intervals; and banal popular music which enters as it were from the outside with a disruptive effect'.

But for most of the music of this period, we have works that are intricately indebted to the past, compete with it directly, or have a pluralistic approach to the combination of available styles, but that nevertheless make the completely autonomous impression of traditional concert music – for example, Ligeti's wonderful *Violin Concerto* (1990/1992). Contemporary composers have been brilliant innovators in the devising of new languages (for example, Ligeti's use of immensely complex polymetric rhythmic sequences, exploitation of the mistunings available from natural harmonics, and so on). The main reason for the distance from postmodernism of this kind of genuinely experimental music is that it is very difficult to make music without words behave like text, or to convey those critical, oppositional, conceptualist messages to be found elsewhere in postmodernist art. The exceptions to this, for example Cage's notorious silent piano composition, *4'33"* (1952), only prove the rule, and in any case have had a short concert-hall life and have been superseded by performance art in art galleries. It is very difficult for music alone to make any kind of political impression except through the very uncertain dialectics of the hearer's allegorical association, as the futile controversies about the anti-Stalinist ironies of Shostakovich's symphonies have shown,

It is in opera and vocal music that we might expect some approximation to postmodernist commitments to be found, but even here there seems to be a loyalty to a coherent, ontologically relatively stable world – as, say, in Turnage's *Greek* (1988), or Birtwhistle's *Mask of Orpheus* (1973–83), or Adès's *Powder Her*

Face (1994–5), or Adams's *Nixon in China* (1987). These are very different from the fictional narratives examined above. An exception to this is Philip Glass's *Einstein on the Beach* (1976), which is a cooperation with the minimalist artist Robert Wilson, and in which no coherent narrative is to be found. The politics of much musical composition in this period has been compatible with the leftist versions of postmodernism, for example in the work of Nono and Henze, but it does not seem by and large that any really significant composers have needed to take on any very explicitly postmodernist theoretical commitments. The most one can say is that, like the postmodernists, composers were often obsessed with the nature and function of language – with its incoherences, with the exploitation of tonal-atonal contradictions, with its hidden but entirely convention-governed structures, and with the ways in which it could be used to deconstruct earlier patterns and procedures.

But this is a very loose relationship to deconstruction as understood in postmodernist theory. You could equally say (and many have) that Cubism 'deconstructed' Impressionism and Post-Impressionism. But this is no more than an analogy, and has no grip on the historical intentions of Picasso and Braque. Very few composers in this period have wasted time in crowing over the 'internal contradictions' of their predecessors. Even Pierre Boulez, a former denouncer of the past ('Schoenberg is dead'), is now conducting Bruckner with the Vienna Philharmonic. At the very least much musical composition since 1970, notably in the extraordinary willingness to mix styles of younger composers, has avoided some of the dialectical battles of the past – Schoenberg versus Stravinsky, theoretical serialism versus chance in the 1950s and 1960s. In this, it owes much to the climate of ideas created by postmodernism.

Art and theory

As I have tried to show, it is the alliance between art and theory which is one of the most obvious symptoms of postmodernist influence. In this respect, it develops the already very strong theoretical line (of 'science', artistic rule or 'law') found in parts of high modernism – in the Bauhaus, twelve-tone music, Le Corbusier, and even, in a far less rigorous and scientific manner, in surrealism. Postmodernist theory has brought into existence a plethora of works of art whose makers and critics are deeply self-conscious about their relationship to language in general and to the previously accepted languages of art in particular. With the rise of academic postmodernism and the growing influence of the political attitudes of the 1960s (both of which actually come after the post-war experimental avant-garde had established many new techniques in the arts), many artists became extraordinarily sensitive about their theoretical, and their political, position. They demanded from the reader and spectator an awareness of a postmodernist metalanguage, which was often needed in order to supplement, complete, and to clothe in critical Emperor's clothes, artworks that were often austere and boring, like the bricks with which we began.

Many modernist works aimed at a kind of self-explanatory autonomy ('all you need to understand' *Four Quartets*, in particular,

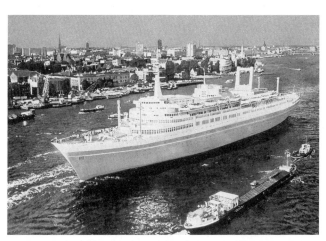

7. *SS Amsterdam in Front of Rotterdam* (1966) by Malcolm Morley. Is this just a big ship, or a statement about the nature of art?

is a continued application to its internal meanings . . . and the widest possible knowledge of 'life', including theology and history) – but postmodernist works were not complete without the critical discussion which was supposed to surround them. It is this *conceptualist self-reflexivity* which is so often the sign of a postmodernist origin. For the postmodernist, to create is to be critically self-aware to an extent that goes far beyond modernism (which is nevertheless responsible for the beginnings of this dire marriage between art and academic elitism). Artist and critic both conspire to demand the 'right' relationship between work and idea, as implied by the creator, and as responded to by the audience.

Conceptualism

We can see how this works if we look at an example – Paul Crowther's classically postmodernist account of Malcolm Morley's huge painting, in oils, of a postcard of the *SS Amsterdam in Front of Rotterdam* (1966).

Morley took a postcard, inverted it, projected it on a screen, covered the projection with a grid, and then copied it, upside down, on a very large scale, even including the white margins of the card. Crowther argues that this 'Super Realism' 'is a critical practice which highlights, questions and thwarts our expectations of art as a "high cultural" activity'. (It does indeed thwart any expectation of a high cultural complexity.) It 'addresses . . . the legitimising discourse whereby art is justified as a vehicle of elevation and improvement'. That is, it does a bit of Foucauldian questioning, though quite what the activity of 'addressing' amounts to remains unclear here, as in most postmodernist uses of this piece of jargon. 'Elevation and improvement' are clearly going to be the 'wrong' kinds of values to expect in this context. But that may still be a pity. No one could possibly think that Morley's ship is elevating or improving. Crowther goes on, 'In Morley's case the critical dimension is as it were painted into the image.' But the weaseling 'as it were' here disguises an impossibility: it is obviously the *critic's*

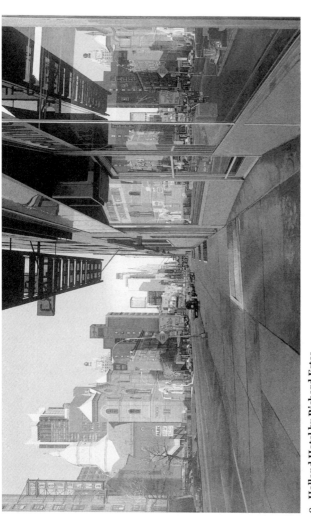

8. Holland Hotel by Richard Estes.
A dangerous formal beauty, retrogressively modernist?

commentary, and not the painting, which is actually providing the 'criticism'. He goes on 'We have not so much a kind of external "anti-art", as art which internalises and displays the problematics of its own socio-cultural status.' Crowther adds that the work of Audrey Flack, Chuck Close, and Duane Hanson has a similar dimension, but that the superficially similar photorealist works of John Salt and Richard Estes are merely 'virtuoso performances' and 'aesthetically dazzling compositions'. He means, presumably, that the latter produce paintings that are enjoyable in a rather traditional way (which, to their advantage, and great formal virtuosity, they are).

Crowther argues that their concentration on such qualities deplorably allowed 'the work of Morley and the other innovators . . . [to be] reappropriated within the legitimising discourse' which surrounds such values. He disapproves of their 'flashy verisimilitude', their 'overwhelming market appeal', and hence their appeal to 'traditional prejudices'. And so in looking like photographs, Estes's work just 'feeds the demand for fashionable novelty and unexpectedness that is created by modernism'. The appreciation of 'aesthetic' or 'virtuoso' qualities is to be thought of as politically regressive, in that it allows us to defend a rather modernist aesthetic *pleasure* in formal composition, of which Crowther clearly disapproves. Indeed, like many other postmodernists, he attacks artists when they show such modernist qualities, which are not 'progressive' by being critical of 'legitimating discourses' including those of modernism. But what then of Crowther's own 'legitimating discourse' – could the work of Estes be construed as a progressive criticism of that? But the work of such artists doesn't really waste much time in criticizing, explicitly or implicitly, other art.

For Crowther, Morley is therefore 'a key artist in understanding the transition from modern to postmodern'. He (and also Kiefer, surprisingly) has the anti-modernist virtues of devising a 'new form of art', and of 'embodying a scepticism as to the posssibility of high art', so that 'By internalising this scepticism and making it

thematic within art practice, *Critical* Super Realism . . .
gives art a *deconstructive* dimension.' It is thus 'definitively '
postmodernist, and the key to this judgement is its 'questioning'
character.

Those who produced conceptual art were easily interpretable as
the true guardians of the postmodernist theorizer's faith. But their
thought is often sloppy by ordinary rational standards, and 'theory'
can too often inhibit the artist from being imaginative or
metaphorically suggestive. You can see what is there pretty quickly,
but what you can't get away from (too quickly) is the theoretical
miasma by which the critic wishes to give it 'significance'. This
work has affinities to, and indeed helped to inspire, postmodernist
thinking because it arises from a self-consciousness about the
theory of art. It was not the object itself but the conceptual
processes behind it that counted. In the process, it took a step
back from the usual activities of art institutions, including those
of selling the object – for example, there was nothing to sell in
Robert Barry's exhibition at the Art and Project Gallery in
Amsterdam in 1969, which consisted in his putting on the gallery
entrance a sign reading 'during the exhibition the gallery will be
closed'.

One consequence of this conceptualism was the loss of a feeling for
complexity in art – the richness of specification of traditional
mimesis and the intriguing formal relationships of modernist art
were often abandoned. The result of this anti-modernist turn could
be a deliberate shallowness, as in much minimalist art, in music as
well as in painting.

Michael Fried argued that a merely literal minimalist object can
only have interest for the spectator as dramatically placed within an
exhibition space, and this contrasts it to its disadvantage with the
modernist mode, in which the spectator is engaged by the
complexity and formal configuration of the object. One mode
demands interaction, the other is a contemplation of internal

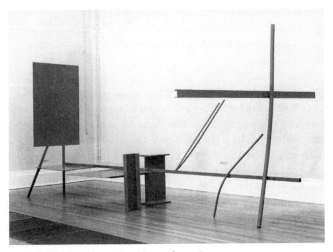

9. *Early One Morning* (1962) by Anthony Caro.
For the contemplative enjoyment of its formal intricacy and self-sufficiency. There are no questions here.

relations. For Fried, the minimalists are mere literalists who rely on our self-awareness as the spectators of art objects, whereas in the modernist internal tradition, we can lose ourselves in absorption in the work of art; this 'theatricality' is at war with modernism. To put it pretty crudely, we enjoy exploring the internal relations of a work sculpted by Anthony Caro; but a heap of felt by Robert Morris offers us no such opportunities, rather it 'poses questions'.

The conceptualism of early artists like Morris and Andre inspired many later postmodernist developments in which the conceptual and the minimal were often combined, to 'ask questions' through quite simple works of art. An example is Michael Craig-Martin's 1973 exhibition of a glass of water on an ordinary bathroom glass shelf, nine feet high on the wall, which he entitles *An Oak Tree*. It was the only object in the exhibition room. Visitors were given an anonymous written questionaire, including:

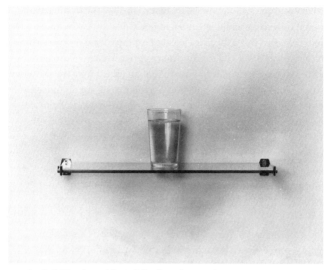

10. *An Oak Tree* (1973) by Michael Craig-Martin.
Sometimes a cigar is just a cigar (Sigmund Freud, attrib.).

Q Haven't you simply called this glass of water an oak tree?

A Absolutely not. It is not a glass of water anymore. I have changed
   its actual substance. It would no longer be accurate to call it a
   glass of water. One could call it anything one wished but that
   would not alter the fact that it is an oak tree . . .

If you've understood even a small bit of the theory discussed in this
book, you might get some of the very small points about the
arbitrariness of naming, the function of the gallery, the joke about
the height of the shelf, and maybe even a little frisson from the
Catholic theology of the Eucharist. All deeply self-conscious, quasi-
intellectual, shallow, surface-oriented, and 'questioning'. But that's
it. In the end, and in the perspective of the last 25 years, and more,
it's just a glass, which depends, as Fried would argue, on not much
more than its theatrical positioning within the institution of the art

gallery and the willingness of art historians like me to refer to it, even if only as an awful example, in books like this. Not much more than that. But it is a far from isolated example, and it does in the dumbest way show the extraordinary pervasiveness of the postmodernist tendency to believe that an allusion to 'theory' along with a bit of 'calling into question' was sufficient, for an indeed minimally significant work of art. Godfrey, from whom I cite the questionnaire, thinks it's a 'clean, simple and elegant installation'. But it's hardly clean, simple, and elegant in the manner of Archipenko or Brancusi or David Smith, or any number of modernist sculptures. But then (back to Fried's theatricality) – it's not exactly a sculpture, though it may resemble one. It's an 'installation'. Just like anyone's DIY bathroom shelf.

The minimalist tendency also emerges in music as a reaction against modernism (but with far better works of art as a result). The simplification here parallels that in visual art; as a reaction against formal complexity, and a declaration that the (twelve-tone, Cubist) obsession with developing the language of art is to be consigned to the elitist values of the past and to alienate those audiences whom the postmodernists wish to address. The minimalist music of Riley Reich, Glass, Nyman, Fitkin, and the later development of the style by John Adams and Michael Torke, makes the distinction between high and low fairly meaningless. The music typically relies upon repetitive rhythmic procedures which do not involve the complexities of language and harmonic development associated with the late modernist music of composers of the 1950s, like Boulez, Henze, and Stockhausen. Many in the musical world indeed thought of minimalist music as being far too banal and simple to be taken seriously. Its early examples relied upon a great deal of perhaps mesmerizing or contemplation-inducing repetition (particularly in the work of Reich, influenced by Zen), and its thematic elements are often very basic and unoriginal (simply intertextual); it was static in harmony and although very complex rhythmically, could seem impersonal.

But works like Reich's *Drumming* (1971) and *Music for 18 Musicians* (1974–6), Adams's opera *Nixon in China* (1987) and his orchestral *Harmonielehre* (1985), changed this. The last of these is a marvellous example of the combination of minimalist technique with a kind of postmodern 'retro' style. This is obvious in the use of allusion to Wagner in the second movement, entitled 'The Amfortas Wound'. This has a chromatic lyricism reminiscent of Schoenberg, and a huge emotional force (which is one of the many things Adams added to the minimalist style). Indeed, Adams's works can build up from essentially simple premises into immensely complex and satisfying structures, which exploit a traditional rhetoric, particularly of stretto and climax, to excite their audiences. Most outrageously so in his *Grand Pianola Music* (1981–2), which produces all that unselfconscious or uncondescending mixture of high and low that the stylistic eclecticism of postmodernism can manage, particularly when in this work Adams introduces 'The Tune', a banal melody that is whipped up into increasingly perverse, grandiose climaxes. All the while, unrelated musical clichés, 'thumping marches, heroic Beethovenian piano arpeggios, ecstatic gospel harmonies – rub shoulders with delirious glee'. Robert Schwarz, whom I cite, goes on to quote Adams as saying that:

> Duelling pianos, cooing female sirens, Valhalla brass, thwacking brass drums, gospel triads and a Niagara of cascading flat keys all learned to cohabit as I wrote the piece.
>
> K. Robert Schwarz, *Minimalists* (1996)

It's as funny as any other work mentioned in this book.

Coming after – and exhaustion?

Many of the innovatory techniques of postmodernist art therefore asked, through artists and the critical establishment, for interpretations that relied on such leading theoretical notions as reflexivity, which arises from the artist's self-consciousness concerning artistic method and ideology, including making the work a critique of previous generic restraints and therefore, in the eyes of many postmodernist critics, of political ones also. An elegant example of an awareness of this 'post' relationship to modernism is to be found in Jeff Wall's *Picture for Women* of 1979, which is a subtle echo of the indirect perspectives of Manet's *Bar at the Folies-Bergere*. Wall, with the release button of his camera in one hand, is staring at the reflection in a mirror of a girl who is posed like Manet's barmaid. This not only makes for an intriguingly complex relationship between the two figures, but is also a witty variation on the indirectness of the 'male gaze' as analysed by feminist critics in this period.

This immense self-awareness also led to the thought that, given the burden of past history (let alone its now suspect mimetic, moral, and political commitments), and the new doctrines concerning intertextuality discussed above, the postmodernist visual artist truly comes 'after' modernism. His or her work is as

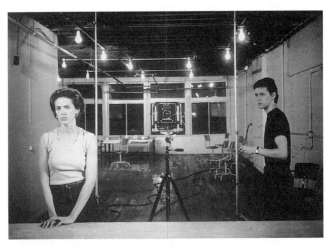

11. *Picture for Women* (1979) by Jeff Wall.
Who looks at whom, at what angle, and why?

much condemned to being a repetition (or 'reinscription', or 'citation') as is the writer's. It is inevitably an intertextual tissue of quotations and adaptations from the past, referring to other works, rather than to any external reality. And so the previously prized, highly individualist, and typically avant-gardist notions of creativity and originality came under attack. Much postmodernist visual art is an apparently easily repeatable, deliberately depthless art of the surface, as we can readily see if we compare, as Jameson does, Andy Warhol's *Diamond Dust Shoes* with the peasants' boots depicted by Van Gogh and seen (by Heidegger) as giving a deep revelatory insight into the world from which they come. For many, postmodernist work can only be hybrid, stylistically mixed, and indebted by resemblance to its predecessors.

One response was to openly affirm one's lack of originality. Douglas Crimp had developed by 1980 a notion of postmodernist photography, based on the work of Cindy Sherman, Sherrie Levine, and Richard Prince, who were praised for:

> showing photography to be always a *re*presentation, always-already-seen. Their images are purloined, confiscated, appropriated, *stolen*. In their work, the original cannot be located, is always deferred; even the self which might have generated an original is shown to be itself a copy.
>
> Douglas Crimp, 'The Photographic Activity of Postmodernism' in
> *October* 15 (1980)

Sherrie Levine thus made photo-reproductions of famous art photos by her male predecessors, like Edward Weston, whose work is thus 'appropriated', in order to 'contest the cult of originality', in the words of Linda Hutcheon. The 'canonic' 'male point of view' is 'put in question' by being *re*produced, and so to speak re-framed, within a female artist's discourse. Rosalind Krauss believes that Levine thus 'radically' questions 'the concept of origin and with it the concept of originality' – in 'violating copyright' by 'pirating'

Walker Evan's photographs of share croppers and Edward Weston's pictures of his son Neil (which, says Krauss, in any case go back, intertextually, to Greek kouroi). Levine's work thus 'explicitly deconstructs the notions of origin' and is 'acting now [it was 1981] to void the basic propositions of modernism, to liquidate them by exposing their fictitious condition'. For Krauss, Levine's 'act' of voiding and liquidating has to be 'located' within a typically postmodern 'discourse of the copy'. But this is another misleading mystification – these images are 'original' only in the manner of bad fakes. To the theoretically unprejudiced eye, they are tatty versions of something better. Just mildly disconcerting. The doubtful morality of such a relationship between artists is nevertheless reassuringly pushed to one side by Krauss's endorsement of Roland Barthes's view that all art is copying anyway. For Barthes has told us that even the painstaking realist only copies copies:

> To depict is to ... refer not from a language to a referent, but from one code to another. Thus realism consists not in copying the real but in copying a (depicted) copy ... Through secondary mimesis [realism] copies what is already a copy.
>
> Roland Barthes, *S/Z* (1974)

The political motivation for this sort of view further emerges when we are told that

> Levine's work may also be seen as a fundamental attack on capitalist notions of ownership and property, along with the patriarchal identification of authorship with the assertion of self-sufficient maleness.
>
> Steven Connor, *Postmodernist Culture* (1989)

But what justifies the word 'fundamental' here? 'Allegorical' or 'pseudo-philosophical' or 'cod profound' may be better expressions.

The attack on originality, and the tendency to think of art as a form of re-presentation of something that is already there, in a recycling of discourse, helped to reinforce the thought of those sceptical about postmodernism, that its art has all too much of a 'post everything' air. May not its intertextuality be the symptom of cultural exhaustion, brought on by the failure to meet the avant-gardist challenge of doing something creatively different after the heroic era of experimental modernism? Or might it even be a moral and political failure to engage with the real in society?

Postmodern architecture

All this promiscuous adaptation can perhaps be seen most clearly in the relationship of postmodernist architecture to the heroic modernism that preceded it. A citational hybridity is typical of much postmodernist work. So much so that in the immensely influential *Learning from Las Vegas* (1972) by Robert Venturi, his wife Denise Scott Brown, and Steven Izenour, Las Vegas architecture and the Strip is praised for its different levels, its use of popular material, and its indifference to unity. Venturi is thinking of the process of looking at the Strip as you drive by it, so that 'the moving eye in the moving body must work to pick out and interpret a variety of changing, juxtaposed orders'. Jencks, in his similarly influential *The Language of Postmodern Architecture* (1977), also argues that the 'codes' in a building (Jencks uses the language of semiotics) should be allowed to come into an ironic conflict of 'double coding' rather like the music by John Adams discussed above.

Much of this happens in Brown and Venturi's Sainsbury Wing (1991) for the National Gallery in London. The architects make allusions to the Corinthian pilasters of the main building, bundling them and then further on spacing them out, so that:

> Although classical elements dominate, they break rules of classical composition in overdetermined ways, with mannerist handling of

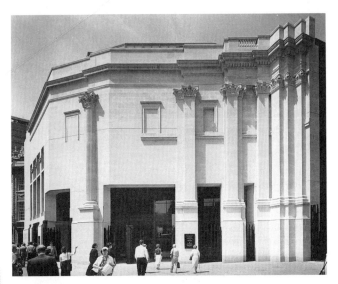

12. Sainsbury Wing, National Gallery, London (1991) by Venturi, Scott Brown and Associates.
A new building, but a pastiche of earlier styles. Is this ironic?

the pilasters, for example, or thoroughly unclassical garage-door-type openings hacked out of the elevation for the entries, windows and loading docks, at once undermining the classical sensibility and contradicting the tectonic logic otherwise so emphatically registered. Each classical detail or abundantly redundant element stands in counterpoint to another that undermines or contradicts classical verities. For Venturi and Scott Brown, contemporary cultural and social diversity calls for an architecture of richness and ambiguity rather than clarity and purity.

Diane Ghirardo, *Architecture after Modernism* (1996)

Architects like Venturi thought that the form-following-function language of modernist architecture was far too puritanical and should allow for the vitality, and no doubt the provocation, to be

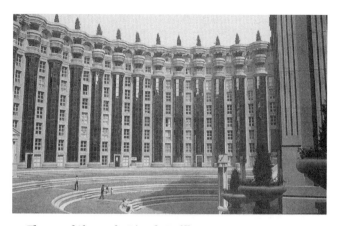

13. Theatre of Abraxas by Ricardo Bofill.
You too can feel small in this postmodernist Palace of Versailles. Fit for a king?

gained from disunity and contradiction. Work like this happily deconstructs itself.

However, such double-coding effects can be, not so much the stimulating and ultimately satisfying combination of stylistic procedures, seen in the National Gallery and Stirling's *Neue Staatsgallerie* in Stuttgart, as a far less sophisticated pop vulgarity. This, at any rate, is what I see in work like Ricardo Bofill's pastiche classical 'Versailles for the Masses' in his *Les Espaces d'Abraxas* in Marne la Vallée (1978–82).

The whole thing is grotesquely inflated. The almost surreal facades here, with their massive columns, conceal modern apartment complexes which are hugely over-burdened with baroque adornment in concrete. It's a kind of pastiche fascist monumental architecture, and it is surprising (or may be not) how much Bofill's work has appealed to local authorities in France. The binary oppositions here are fairly obvious, but human scale and human dignity and convenience are as little cared for here as they were at the opposite pole, in the austerely subordinating modernist work of Le Corbusier.

Discourse and power

There was a growing politicization of the postmodernist avant-garde in the 1970s and 1980s. Most artists knew some version of the Foucauldian relationship between discourse and power, and this often took the form of an awareness of the ways in which the 'messages' or the semiotics of works of art fitted or not within the institutions designed to promote them. This led to a critique of the dependence of art on 'the museum-gallery complex' (as if it were rather like the 'military-industrial complex'). The notion is that the museum, as a kind of secular temple, 'legitimizes' the work through the discourse of a pseudo-clergy of curators and their dependent critic-reviewers. But it is the way in which they pick the team of artists, and write the catalogues, that really counts, and their willingness in this period to allow the enemy of critique within depended a good deal upon the intellectual shield of academic theory.

Hence the conception and use of the work of art as institutional critique, though this very quickly acquired the rather tired air of preaching to the converted. One of the most literal-minded of such 'critiques' was made by Michael Asher, who in 1973 sandblasted a wall of the Toselli Gallery in Milan, thus collapsing 'the work' and 'the gallery' into one another, 'so as to reveal at once their collusion and the strong but usually unacknowledged power of the gallery's invisibility as a dominant (and dominating) cultural institution' – presumably, simply because once Toselli had blasted through the picture gallery wall, you could see the administrative offices behind it.

Slightly more subtle, perhaps, is some of the work of Hans Haacke concerning the museum gallery complex. He has specialized, amongst other things, in the documentation of the economic fortunes of works of art. One of his works (1975) consists of a reproduction of Seurat's 'Les Poseuses' and 14 chronologically arranged panels, each of which has where available a small printed portrait of each successive owner of the image, along with a brief biography.

The spectator was therefore expected to look – or rather to think – beyond the walls of the gallery space, to the social circumstances of the work of art, just as literary students were exhorted to look beyond the closed aesthetic practices of practical or 'new' criticism, and to consider the social context of the work of literature. Here's the classic and orthodox view of this:

> In the radical clime of the time, it was not surprising that the major contradictions which constituted the social sphere of late capitalism should have come to motivate the production of critical art.
>
> Paul Wood et al., *Modernism in Dispute* (1993)

These 'major contradictions', of course, are not just logical ones, ripe for deconstruction – they are Marxist contradictions, significant of the repressed and hidden conflicts within society. Those who attended a show of 'The New Photography' were therefore encouraged to ask:

> Why is such an such an image significant? How does it manage to signify? Why does a society require certain images at particular times? Why do genres arise in photography? How and why do particular images become judged aesthetically worthy? Why do photographers produce pictures which, above and beyond their technical wizardry or creative acumen, say something about the social world? What are the political meanings of photography? Who controls the machinery of photography in contemporary society?
>
> Linda Hutcheon, *The Politics of Postmodernism* (1989)

The same excellent questions were being asked of all the arts – of novels and poems, and pieces of music. Critics were hostile to the lack of (their own) political insight in the art of the past, and this prompted creative people in all the media to produce a good deal of rather nervous, 'politically correct' art, which was either explicitly or by theoretical implication in favour of obviously good political issues. They did not just attack the idea of art as the expensively enjoyable possession of the 'bourgeois' rich (for example, by producing simple, cheap, ugly, and so 'market-defying' conceptual objects), but produced art which, in tune with the ethic outlined earlier, supported feminism, or the marginal group, or proclaimed identities based on gender, sexual orientation, and ethnic origins.

Much of the political art of the modernist period, and certainly that produced by totalitarian regimes, had been boringly realist and only too obviously subordinated to totalizing ideologies. But the political art of postmodernism, devoted as it was to 'differance', 'calling into question', and suchlike, could be much more reassuringly 'avant-garde' in a way that symbolized dissent, rather than making any demands for group solidarity. The moral appeal to us to recognize the autonomy of the 'other' was thus transformed by postmodernism into very fragmented proclamations of marginality and difference, the 'deconstruction' of dominant attitudes, attacks on stereotypical judgements, and so on. These stereotypes were often challenged by their proclamation in a parody form – as, for example, in Lynda Benglis's controversial photographs of herself naked, including one (of 1974) in which she posed as a pin-up girl wearing dark glasses and holding a massive double-ended dildo. This was probably meant to be parodic, a put-on or take-off, of media stereotypes, but like so much art of this kind, it also *uses* them. It's a sexy picture appealing to men. The same double-effect is to be found in literary parody, such as the playfully combinatorial pornographic writing which exploits stereotype to be found in experimental novels from Robbe-Grillet's *La maison de rendezvous* (1965) to Robert Coover's *Gerald's Party* (1986).

I'll consider feminist work in what follows as my central examples, because it often has the advantage of being immersed in postmodernist theory, and the (rather contrary) advantage of having fairly clear ethical ends in view. In the earlier part of this period, much of this art was simple political proclamation, for example Faith Wilding's *Waiting* (1972), a performance piece in which she sat on a chair and recited the events for which women wait. Or Martha Rosler's *Semiotics of the Kitchen* (1975), a video in which she recites the alphabet, illustrating the use of kitchen implements to exemplify each letter, but ends up by slicing the air with a knife.

Much of the feminist art of the early 1970s was later attacked for its 'essentialist' approach, that is for making assumptions about the differences between the sexes that ignored the postmodernist emphasis on the more fluid, socially constructed nature of identity. *The Dinner Party* (1973–9), made by Judy Chicago and others, is a good example. This was a triangular table with an open centre and 39 place settings. These consist of an elaborate ceramic china plate, a needlework runner, a ceramic chalice, a knife, fork, and spoon. Each is a symbolic portrait of a mythological or historically significant woman. The plates are in the form of (butterfly-like) vaginas. The interior floor has 2,300 tiles with 999 additional names. Four hundred women helped to make it, and it has become a central work within feminist art history. It symbolizes neatly the feminist drive to historical recovery and it also contests the male-dominated pantheon by providing an alternative. But its rather kitschy manufacture and style was thought by some to undercut its more serious aims; and isn't there a disturbing 'essentialism' involved in allowing vulvic imagery to stand for women?

The use of this imagery was also to be defended as a reply to common and Freudian-inspired notions of women as somehow 'lacking' the phallus and its powerful connotations (a notion which in itself makes amazingly perverse and misogynistic assumptions,

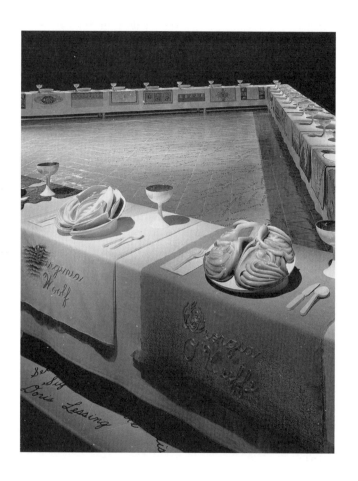

14. *The Dinner Party* (1979) by Judy Chicago.
A feminist symposium: but are the identities of the participants constrained by the imagery used to 'represent' them?

which Freud seems to have derived from Schopenhauer and others, about the essential unimportance of female sexual responses). For others, it was too much of a reduction of women to their biology. The choice of responses here clearly depends on the battle you think you are fighting, and has little to do with the merits of *The Dinner Party* as a pantheon.

Another example of an essentialist approach to feminist art is to be found in the performance work of Carolee Schneeman, whose performance, *Interior Scroll*, of 1975 is well described by David Hopkins: it

> involved her standing naked before an audience and gradually unravelling a scroll from her vagina. From this she read a parodic account of a meeting with a 'structuralist film maker' who had criticised her films for their 'personal clutter' and 'persistence of feelings'. In a sense Schneeman's performance dealt with the internalisation of criticism, but it could also be aligned with an 'essentialist' feminist interest in *écriture féminine* (female writing). This form of French feminist theory, espoused by writers such as Helene Cixous, posited female access to a pre-Oedipal (hence implicitly anti-patriarchal) 'language;' of bodily pulsations.
>
> David Hopkins, *After Modern Art: 1945–2000* (2000)

Indebted to popular art, but more indirect in its emphases, is the later work of Cindy Sherman, for example her *#228* (1990), which is a kitschy, huge photographic representation of the biblical Judith – popular, even cinematic in style. It parodies large Renaissance oil paintings of this subject, which (with the magnificent exception of a painting by Artemisia Gentileschi) would typically have expressed the 'high culture' of men, and no doubt some of their castration anxieties as well. Sherman said that she wanted to make something that 'anybody off the street could appreciate . . . I wanted to imitate something out of the culture, and also make fun of the culture as I was doing it'. For postmodernist feminists, work like this 'raises issues', such as those of 'masquerade and female identity, feminine

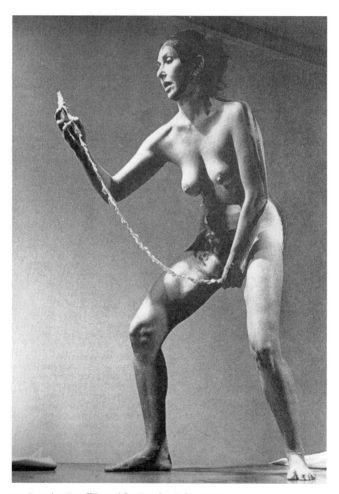

15. *Interior Scroll* (1975) by Carolee Schneeman.
We write with the body, but with what sense can women's writing also
come from the body?

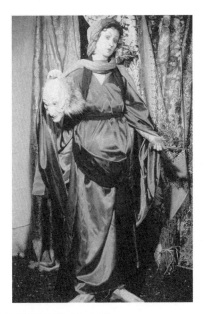

16. *Untitled, #228* (1990) by Cindy Sherman.
Acting out and the threat of castration: is Judith's story also Cindy Sherman's?

stereotypes in visual representation, the gendered viewer, the female body and fetishism, his-story and her-story etc.', as Wood puts it. (But for others, not having the theory to make this kind of interpretation, it may do far less.)

Rather more complex, and more obviously theoretical, is the photographic work of Barbara Kruger. She took photos from magazines, enlarged them, cropped them, spliced them, and combined them with text, in ways which reflected her experience as a magazine designer. The photomontage is then photographed as a whole and typically surrounded by a (Rodchenko-like) red frame. These are parody advertisements, designed to provoke a critique of 'the relations between commercial design and the way a culture designs people's lives', as Kruger explained to *The New York Times*. They help us to understand how images work in society, in a feminist critique of representation, because they are images of women as they are constructed by the male-dominated media, which shape the way women see themselves. Work like this is intended to expose stereotypes that perpetuate the prevailing power balance between women and men. In doing so, it contests the active 'male gaze', and empowers the hitherto passive female gaze. This is symbolized in another of Kruger's images (*Untitled*, 1981) of a classical female bust, seen from the side, with the slogan 'Your gaze hits the side of my face'. This has a designed ambiguity. Whose gaze? Any man's? Why 'hits'? Against what – the male, classical, canonized view of women, as expressed in sculpture? And so on. The texts on other images also help to deconstruct, in the crude sense of 'show the contradictions in', the assumptions of consumerism. For example, 'Buy me I'll change your life' (1984) or 'I shop therefore I am' (1987).

However, it has been pointed out that Kruger's photographs get themselves into their own contradictions (from some feminist points of view), because they are as seductive as the commercial advertising they parody. They have been attacked for a consequent failure to be sufficiently politically effective. Are they a critique of the consumerist spectacle or a part of it? There is a good old-fashioned modernist formal achievement here, and so Kruger has also been attacked for the 'graphic beauty' of her work, let alone for showing it in a commercial gallery.

The options here are as I suggested earlier: either to come within dominant discourses and try to modify them from within, or to accept and proclaim marginalization, and attempt to make the edge move into the centre.

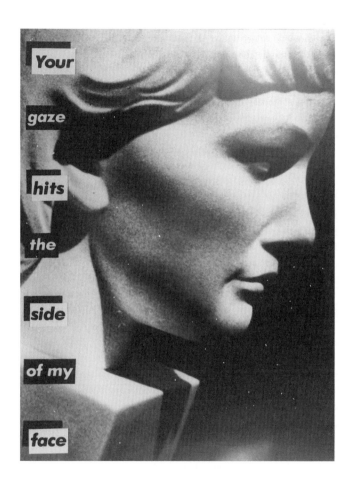

17. *Untitled (Your gaze hits the side of my face)* (1981) by
Barbara Kruger.
Art with a message: how violent is the male gaze?

Art as politics

Nearly all the works of art I have mentioned have the critical, oppositional character I have emphasized. But they seem to have needed, indeed solicited, the institutional support of the critic to get anywhere. Benjamin Buchloh is one of many who tell us that:

> another function of criticism at this moment [is] to support and expand knowledge of those artistic practices of resistance and opposition which are currently developed by artists outside the view of the hegemonic market and of institutional attention.
>
> Benjamin Buchloh, 'Theories of Art after Minimalism and Pop' in H. Foster (ed.), *Discussions in Contemporary Culture* (1987)

But this won't entirely do. The work of art alone, on the wall, or in the gallery space, or even out there as 'earth art' or 'site art', isn't actually a very good participant (and therefore not a particularly good ally for the critic) in a political debate. This is because debate, as opposed to propaganda, requires two sides, not one, and sides which are both able to give clear and articulate reasons for their positions, and it is the negotiation of conflict which makes for real progress as opposed to merely conceptual sloganizing. Thus, one might say that Kruger remains tied to bourgeois priorities, in so far as she really only asks for individual empowerment; and that much of this politically correct work, like Haacke's, although it seems to 'address' the wider issues of economic control and social justice, does little more than remind us that there are good guys and bad guys, and that some of the bad ones are male, or art dealers, property developers, the directors of large corporations, arms dealers, and so on.

All this of course depends on where you think the most useful locus for political debate and action is to be found. Some postmodern artists and theorists (and some feminists like those who say 'the personal is the political') answer 'everywhere'. But visual artists rarely *inform* people about politics by making political 'statements' (though they can), and generally say or imply very simple things to the already converted. Their work has nothing like the sophistication in this respect of even the most popular mass work of political art with the benefit of actual dialogue, such as Spielberg's film *Schindler's List*. If political action is to depend on rhetorical persuasion, the postmodern visual arts have been signally unable to provide that persuasion – except occasionally by the tired old propagandistic techniques of prodding information into us through basic mimetic means, even if occasionally with the sauce of irony. As Marxist critics of postmodernism never tire of telling us, it is realist art which by expressing a particular critical position on reality still has by far the best record for being effectively progressive, precisely because it can to some degree inform as well as attempt to persuade. But as we have seen, such explicit methods do not appeal to the postmodernist criteria for the politics of representation in this period.

Or to put it more robustly, as Robert Hughes does: 'What really changes political opinion is events, argument, press photographs, and TV.' Artists may be 'addressing issues' of racism, sexism, AIDS, etc. . . . but

> an artist's merits are not a function of his or her gender, ideology, sexual preference, skin colour, or medical condition, and to address an issue isn't necessarily to address a public . . . The Political art we have in America is one long exercise in preaching to the converted.

> Robert Hughes, *Culture of Complaint* (1993)

Hughes is also right to point out that the problem with much of such political art is that its ideas aren't actually much good – they are often banal and naive, and they put no one through any very unusual or sophisticated thought process. For example, 'a work by Jessica Diamond consisting of an equals sign cancelled out with a cross, underneath which was lettered in a feeble script "Totally

Unequal". Anyone who thinks that this plaintive diagram contributes anything fresh to one's grasp of privilege in the United States merely by virtue of getting some wall space in a museum is dreaming'. At best, such art 'consists basically of taking an unexceptional if obvious idea – "racism is wrong" . . . . – then coding it so obliquely that when the viewer has translated it he feels the glow of being included in what we call the "discourse" of the art world'. (Robert Hughes, op. cit.)

The work of art might criticize society and its institutions, but it all the same ends up being exhibited in that society, sold by a dealer, and generally legitimated by the opinions of a middle-class art establishment. It didn't prevent a bid of $90,000 by Gilbert Silverman for a work by Haacke, *Social Grease*, although the work mocks major corporate and political figures by quoting their words, on a separate metal plaque, as advocating the arts as a 'social lubricant'. This is less of a paradox than it seems. Liberal societies have spent over a century absorbing artworks that are hostile to them. In general, and with notorious exceptions, such societies do not neutralize or censor artists, but protect their right to expression. (Though occasionally the illiberal members of a liberal society attempt to upset this assumption, as in the Mapplethorpe scandal, when federal funding for the exhibition of some of his gay sadomasochistic photographs was contested.)

Nevertheless, the basic legal and social structures in the societies I am writing about here are emphatically liberal ones. Even if it is the institution and not the work of art that first claims legitimacy, after that, it is the long-run value to the observer of the individual work of art that counts, far beyond the 'statement' of any one show. There is nothing more boring and dated than the last few decades' conceptualist and feminist news. Explicitly doctrinal, postmodernist work often looks disablingly academic in this sense. There is a bigger difference between doctrinal postmodernism and the kind of contemporary art that can provide an intellectual simulus over a long period than many postmodernist critics seem to appreciate. Of course, works of art should 'call into question' – what else does the tradition of tragedy from *Antigone* to the *Hedda Gabler* do? But they need to do so in far more complex and enduring ways than we find in most recent postmodernist art.

The postmodernist theory that many in the avant-garde went for was a version of the philosophy, along with its politics and history, that I have outlined in previous sections. Privilege and its hierarchically organized terms, including the formalism associated with modernism, were to be attacked and subverted. Ordered narrative and the centre, and transcendental terms of value, were to be distrusted. The primacy of Western culture (and any privileged ordering by reference to it) also had to be doubted. The aim often enough was morally admirable: to look to the margin, to the repressed, to the excluded, and to argue for a subversion or reversal of dominant values. This was indeed a classic liberal impulse, but it took place under shaky theoretical auspices. For example, it is unclear, despite Derrida's latest thoughts, whether truly deconstructive work like his *can* have anything like a settled and effective political position.

The visual arts had also caught up to the paradoxical thought that *everything* was potentially 'text'. This textualizing view of the world, typical of Derrida and Barthes, dominated on the assumption that all thinking was somehow in language. And this left out a good part of our non-linguistic responses to previous art – such as simply enjoying the texture of the paint, or the colour, or formal relationships – either as a dismissible hangover from the hedonism of a decadent formalist modernism, or as in need of salvation by the laying-on of some suitably theoretical conceptual-verbal association. Everything, from furniture to clothes to buildings, had to be seen as part of a 'language' whose social structure could be investigated and then shown to be susceptible to some kind of disruption or reversal, away from the suspect hierarchical ordering it had received in a 'bourgeois' society. And if everything was part of a language, and if language just disseminates, and if the discourses of art, like the discourses of medicine, law, penology, and so on, actually transcend the individual, then even the notions of authorship, creativity, originality were suspect and could not be 'privileged'.

This generously democratizing impulse, which saw the reader and student swimming in exactly the same linguistic sea as the great novelist, and so *equally* in a position to dominate the text by interpretation, was spread, ironically enough, by some highly authoritarian, idiosyncratic, and well-paid cultural critics. The explanation of the artwork through the individual temperament or the experience that produced it, or the aspect of reality that it tried to record, was out.

Hence, for example, the postmodernist attacks on the 'neo-expressionist' painting of the 1980s. This conflict is worth analysing because it shows that there were active rival traditions to postmodernism, and that some leading postmodernists attacked them in explicitly political terms. Not only was neo-expressionist painting from Germany and the United States 'painterly', expressive, and clearly emotional, but it 'privileged' the old-fashioned, hierarchizing concept of painting itself.

For it was quite obvious that American neo-expressionists, like Julian Schnabel, David Salle, and Eric Fischl, were allied or similar to European artists like Sandro Chia, Francisco Clemente, Georg Baselitz, Jorg Immendorff, Anselm Kiefer, and P. A. R. Penck, who obviously went back to modernist German expressionism. What is more, they extended, rather than subverted or parodied or 'critiqued' it. In so doing, they brought back a sensuousness and emotionalism to art which had been banished by the puritanism of postmodernist theory. We can interpret Fischl, for example, as an expressionist figurative painter, on psychological grounds that need owe nothing to postmodernism, even if the rather skewed psychology and apparent alienation of his characters obviously

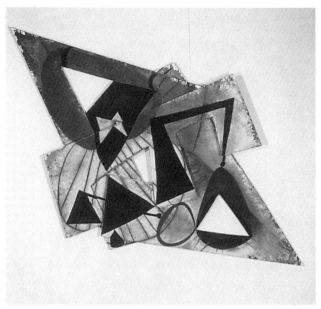

18. *Her Story* (1984) by Elizabeth Murray.
Can postmodernist themes of identity be reconciled with modernist modes of expression?

owes something to the more general postmodernist climate of ideas concerning narrative. Similarly, painters like Jennifer Bartlett, Robert Colescott, Nicholas Africano, and Elizabeth Murray could be seen as reviving rather than subverting past traditions in modernist painting. They allowed themselves the risks of more direct competition and extension of the past – one can see Bartlett as a successor to Monet, for example.

The neo-expressionists, and the abstract painters defended by the critic Barbara Rose, were attacked by the postmodernist October group, who announced 'The End of Painting' in an article by Douglas Crimp (in 1981). Crimp thought Rose's appeal to a continuous (modernist) tradition was 'reactionary'. It was

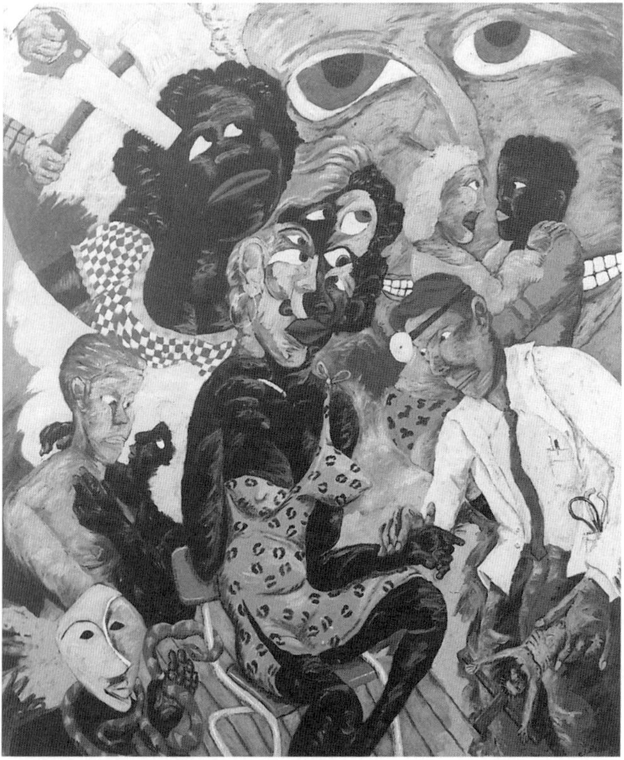

19. ***Grandma and the Frenchman (Identity Crisis)*** **(1990) by Robert Colescott.**
And doesn't the expression of personal identity demand an imposed narrative and a realist mode?

> in direct opposition to that art of the sixties and seventies . . . which sought to contest the myths of high art, to declare art, like all other forms of endeavour, to be contingent upon the real, historical world.

Crimp also attacked in this context 'the myth of man and the ideology of humanism which it supports', because they 'are notions that sustain the dominant bourgeois culture. They are the very hallmarks of bourgeois ideology'. Neo-expressionist painting was therefore attacked for being politically conservative, because artists shouldn't therefore think of constructing alternative and pleasurable worlds in works of art; they should ask how the world and its discourses had constructed them, and preferably come to the conclusion that it had constructed them as victims. Postmodernist critics were more important than art or artists, since they operated on what was for them an acceptable institutional or political level, even though it should have been obvious to anyone with any sense that the primarily academic techniques they were using were really quite basic, and easy to come by, given a decent education and a certain rhetorical persuasiveness. This was far less than the talent needed to produce significant art of any kind in earlier periods. But the main thing was to set up a critical opposition, bolstered by current theory. Much postmodernist criticism can be seen as the academy's political revenge upon the central traditions and pleasures of art, and therefore, as I shall argue, the defence of a very narrow tradition within the extraordinarily various visual, musical, and literary art of this period. It is to this broader context that I now turn.

Chapter 5
The 'postmodern condition'

Confidence in truth

One of the central themes of all that has gone before might be summarized as 'realism lost', and along with it a reliable sense of past history. Indeed, Frederic Jameson points to a defining sense of the postmodern as 'the disappearance of a sense of history' in the culture, a pervasive depthlessness, a 'perpetual present' in which the memory of tradition is gone. For many postmodernists there was something in the very condition of society that brought this about.

As we have seen, much postmodernist analysis is an attack on authority and reliability – in philosophy, narrative, and the relationship of the arts to truth. All this sceptical activity has a complex relationship, not just to the attitudes of academics and artists, but to what was seen as a more general loss of confidence within Western democratic culture. Left-wing hostility to the hidden manipulations of 'late capitalism', and the quite general belief, even among the most optimistic of liberals, that real news is too often subordinated to image manipulation, that the dissemination of basic information is always distorted by business corporate interests, and that even horrifyingly immediate events, which cause unimaginable suffering to individuals, like the Vietnam and Gulf wars, had become in some way just 'dramatized media events' which 'take place on TV' in scenes constructed for political ends by the cameras – the sniper with the camera over his shoulder, the speech-makers' hopes for the better on the White House lawn, and so on. There is a strong feeling, through the work of critics like Barthes to the novels of Milan Kundera and Rushdie, that the political and historical event always reaches us in a fictionalized form, in a narrative, massaged by the more or less hidden hand of political or economic purposes.

It is not difficult to appreciate how well TV works as the chief disseminator of such fictionalized information. There is so much of it, it is so contradictory, so obviously motivated by ('hegemonic') economic interests, so commodified, so much to be distrusted. It's an obvious target, because the medium seems to rely on the realist 'transparent' presentation which we associate with photography, and this very fact invites postmodernist scepticism.

Unreal images

This feeling that the mass media substitute images for reality arises in various ways, from the Marxist presupposition that we are all in any case the victims of a 'false consciousness' brought about by 'bourgeois' discourse, through to the liberal distrust of corporate restraints on free speech. The problem is that this attack on truthful realism – ever since, indeed, the moderns turned against that of the 19th century – has by now gone on so long that for many a distrust of the fictional has indeed driven out a confidence in the true, as we saw in the controversy over the writing of history. Jameson, as a Marxist, likes the thought that there is a general 'crisis of representation'. His idea is that with postmodernity, signs have been relieved of their function of referring to the world, and 'this brings about the expansion of the power of capital into the realm of the sign, of culture and representation, along with the collapse of modernism's prized space of autonomy'. We are left

with that pure and random play of signifiers which we call postmodernism, which no longer produces monumental works of the modernist type, but ceaselessly reshuffles the fragments of pre-existent texts, the building blocks of older cultural and social production [in a] heightened bricolage: metabooks which cannibalise other books, metatexts which collate bits of other texts.

Frederic Jameson,'Postmodernism and the Video Text' in Derek Attridge et al. (eds), The Linguistics of Writing (1987)

For many postmodernists, we live in a *society of the image*, primarily concerned with the production and consumption of mere 'simulacra'. Information, by now, is just something that we buy. (And perhaps the main thing that we buy, in a knowledge-dominated technologically driven society.) We are always trying to learn a new bit of software. A sceptical despair about the reality of politics and the institutions of our common social life – TV and newspapers – reinforces a sceptical despair about the progressive or conciliatory functions of art. The Nietzschean assumption that all such phenomena, from statements from the White House to everyday soap operas, are more or less secretly in the service of the maintenance of the power, economic and other, of somebody or other, rather than made in the service of any truth, is all-pervasive. It has led to a peculiarly paranoid strain in postmodernist theory and art, as well as in those popular films concerned with real or fictional conspiracies. How many people believe that Oliver Stone's film *JFK*, which presents us with a New Orleans attorney heroically confronting those in the military establishment who conspired to assassinate Kennedy in order to keep the United States fighting in Vietnam, is not the fiction it is, but the truth?

Perhaps the most celebratedly outrageous assertion of the essential unreality of the culture in which we live was made by Jean Baudrillard, who echoed Foucault in arguing that

> Disneyland is there to conceal the fact that it is the 'real' country, all of 'real' America, which *is* Disneyland (just as prisons are there to

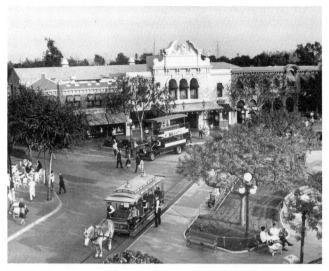

20. The Imagineers *Main Street USA* (1955) Anaheim, California. Is this the street where you live?

conceal the fact that it is the social; in its entirety, in its banal omnipresence, which is carceral).

He goes on to say that Disneyland (with its Pirates, Frontier, and Future World fantasy set-ups)

is presented as imaginary in order to make us believe that the rest is real, when in fact all of Los Angeles and the America surrounding it are no longer real, but of the order of the hyperreal and of simulation. It is no longer a question of a false representation of reality (ideology), but of concealing the fact that the real is no longer real, and thus of saving the reality principle.

The Disneyland imaginary is neither true nor false; it is a deterrence machine set up in order to rejuvenate in reverse the fiction of the real.

Jean Baudrillard, *Simulations* (1983)

We are simply enclosed in a media-dominated world of signs, villainously generated by capitalism to synthesize our desires, which only really refer to one another within an entrapping chain of ideas. They are mere simulacra, which replace real things and their actual relationships (only truly known to those on the left, who see through such illusions) in a process which Baudrillard calls 'hyperrealization'. So we never really get what we want anyway. But we might on the contrary say that we do indeed get what we pay for, however it is advertised – a McDonald's hamburger is a McDonald's hamburger in all its billions of exemplifiers, and to many it really does taste pretty good. And if you smell of Dune perfume you smell of Dune perfume. All this is not *mere* sign-play, however much advertising might try to induce us to buy into it. But even those of us who have not read any postmodernist theory are not completely taken in, and don't really believe that anybody else is, much. Read the opinion polls on politicians worldwide. Or even market research on the effects of advertising. But to hear Baudrillard and others like him, you would think we ate, drank, and slept on and with mere signifiers. Up to a point. This sort of argument combines the old liberal attack on advertising (as synthesizing wants that we don't 'really' have), with a bit of pessimistic Freudianism – signs for objects always deceive, and one can never get back through them to the 'really' desired object. A replica of the Lascaux Caves in France has displaced the real Lascaux – it really makes no difference, we are asked to believe. But even the most naive of Lascaux's visitors could easily be made to understand how they, let alone an art historian, can tell the difference between the real and a fake, and also even to understand conservationist reasons, if there are any, for the use of a replica for tourists.

Postmodernists are by and large pessimists, many of them haunted by lost Marxist revolutionary hopes, and the beliefs and the art they inspire are often negative rather than constructive. Mass affluence is not good, because when people have what they basically need, advertising and marketing move into the gap to synthesize and define our (materialist) values for us, and those who do need are the more easily forgotten. Marketing thus takes precedence over production. We have the sense that even justice is or can become a media event – as in the trial of O. J. Simpson shown on TV, so clearly influenced by the exaggerated play-acting of advocates, the carefully chosen clothing of the actors in the drama, and the politically slanted, stereotypically prejudiced sound-bite summaries of lawyers and TV journalists. The whole thing can seem sickeningly fictional, as all participants manipulate opinion, through the media, by hypocritically approximating themselves to what they believe to be approved role models and fictional stereotypes. We may well ask, how is justice of a disinterested kind to be done on such a stage? Are judge and jury, who are after all in the end only one of us, really going to be taken in by all this shameless role-playing? Or are the procedures of justice in court somehow to be thought of as more reliable than that? There is room for doubt about this in all of us, and it is that doubt that postmodernists (and, indeed, the writers of many court-room thrillers) rightly insist upon.

But they also tend to give a misleadingly pessimistic account of the information we receive and of conflict and its resolution. Many of them in fact belong to a long post-Nietzschean tradition of despair about reason. In correctly seeing all discourses as inherently related to the power systems that might be thought to back them up – as expressing power – they can give the impression that our culture is not much more than a complex interaction of opposing threats of force. Their scepticism about truth often deprives them of a proper concern for the activities of reason-giving and rational negotiation and for procedural justice. The background influence of Marx and Freud too often implies that everything we say carries the authority and the threat of race, class, rank, and sexual power-play. But this hardly allows for the function in democratic societies of legal agreements and restraints, or of the moral considerations that lead to the protection of human rights which really are meant to be universal and not culturally relative or the property of any one group. Nor does it allow for the fact that the attempt to be reasonable, and truthful, to back up assertions by verifiable evidence, and so on, is essential if we are to come to the negotiating table with something other than implied threats (or to treat the writing of history or theology or the novel as something better than the entrapment of the reader in a mythical narrative). Imagine someone who thought that anything that any (American, or Israeli, or Russian, and other) politician said was always a form of imperialist, or theological, or 'rogue state' bullying, simply because it implicitly reflected, say, the power of that nation's political institutions and armed forces.

Of course, many proclamations by such persons indeed do this, to horrifying effect, but particularly in cases of conflict it may be all the more important to locate the voices of the most reasonable persons – for example those who are most open to a rational conviction concerning the guilt and responsibility that arises out of conflict.

The best that one can say here, and I am saying it, is that postmodernists are good critical deconstructors, and terrible constructors. They tend to leave that job to those patient liberals in their society who are still willing to attempt to sort out at least some of those differences between truth and fantasy, which postmodernists blur in a whirlwind of pessimistic assumptions about the inevitability of class or psychological conflict.

On the other hand, postmodernists have clearly reflected to great purpose on the nature of cultural changes since 1945 into what they call the 'postmodern condition'. This is one in which the global condition of societies is seen, not as determined by traditional economic or political frameworks, but as a *state of culture*. This reliance upon a cultural analysis (now given prominence by a flourishing 'cultural studies' movement heavily influenced so far by postmodernist ideas) is one of the most distinctive contributions of postmodernism to contemporary society. The activities of 'late capitalism' and of Western democracies are obviously going concerns, with no obvious alternative to them currently available (certainly since 1989). Given a general, even if illusory, presumption of continued plenty, they are seen by postmodernists as primarily information-producing rather than object-producing formations, which demand analysis primarily in cultural terms.

A postmodernist view of the social changes that have most affected contemporary society would therefore (and I broadly follow David Harvey here) emphasize such matters as the extraordinary compression of time and space through the new media. (We can now get simultaneous access via TV and the Internet to events and information in nearly any part of the world.) The Internet is at present a typically postmodernist phenomenon – it is (currently) a non-hierarchized, indeed disorganized, collage. This goes along with a change from a concentration on the production of goods, to a concentration on the production of information services. (The story here is that huge fortunes are made or lost every day, not in buying or selling things, but by operations in the money market by traders in front of TV screens which give them computerized access to more information than ever was available before.) For some this is a symptom of the scandalous superimposition of fluctuating news images or opinion (that of the 'market makers') over reality, but this is again typical of the 'postmodern condition'. Many of us are working in an incredibly driven, information-soaked world (and those of us who are not are often starving or illiterate or struggling at the bottom of the social heap or mentally ill). There is too much of everything. We are subject everywhere to a sensory overload of images, in magazines and advertisements, on the TV, in the cityscape, etc. (This was a modernist complaint, too.) Mere changes in taste promote the sale of goods, so that fashion takes over from culture, and media-led opinion-forming is vital to the economic process.

In all of this diagnosis, postmodernists are open to the charge that they seriously overestimate the gullibility of their fellow-citizens. Many of their strictures are sheer nannying about the obvious, which hardly merits its respectable disguise in the shreds of theory. And for some, this state of affairs is OK. In the post-McLuhanite global village in which we all now more or less live, held together by electronic contact rather than by genuine social relationships between persons, *of course* signs may come to count for more than commodities.

It is worth asking, then, how far a postmodernist 'hermeneutics of suspicion' is justified. There is in any case a crippling contradiction at the heart of the analysis – if anyone says that everything is 'really' just constituted by a deceiving image, and not by reality, how does he or she *know*? They presuppose the very distinctions they attack. At best, such critics are making a banal and condescending series of remarks about *other people's* (self-)deceit, or merely deploring, on well-established liberal moral grounds, the success of the advertising industry, TV, etc. in getting people to consume and to believe things of which they (the critics) disapprove. This is no more distinctive a view than a preference for the views of one politician over another, and it is hardly good evidence for original insight into a radically new condition of contemporary society.

The more basic problem lies in the undoubted decline, for a significant minority, of assent to previously popular orthodoxies and ideologies. A postmodernist sceptic, noting the extraordinary range of conflicting versions of reality available to us within a remarkably tolerant and pluralist society, and willing to be a bit of a relativist, might well be inclined to opt for something like Richard Rorty's *postmodernist irony*. Such ironists have doubts about the truth of any 'final vocabulary', and realize that others have different ones; they don't see their vocabulary as 'closer to reality' than other people's. They can only worry that they may be playing the wrong kind of language game, and so be the wrong kind of human being. Such a person

> is not in the business of supplying himself and his fellow ironists with a method, a platform, or a rationale. He is just doing the same thing that all ironists do – attempting autonomy. He is trying to get out from under inherited contingencies and make his own

contingencies, get out from under an old final vocabulary and fashion one which will be all his own. The generic trait of ironists is that they do not hope to have their doubts about their final vocabularies settled by something larger than themselves. This means that their criterion for resolving doubts, their criterion of private perfection, is autonomy rather than affiliation to a power other than themselves.

Richard Rorty, *Contingency, Irony and Solidarity* (1989)

The idea here is that an awareness of the lack of foundations and the contingency of everything is a good thing. It would be more liberal because discussion of what is possible would be the less constrained, along with an awareness that one's own position in such discussions is relative, in the sense that the opposition's view may be as well founded. This is for Rorty a kind of existential irony. The ironist has doubts about the vocabulary he or she uses; others' vocabularies also seem to work well. These doubts cannot be removed by any 'final answer' or foundational position; you can always doubt whether others have not seen more of reality than you can (with your vocabulary). Or in the artistic rather than the philosophical or political or moral spheres, we can say that there are lots of ways of making art, and no one privileged way of interpreting it. Indeed, philosophy should be a good deal more like literary or artistic criticism than it thinks it is. So the irony really consists in our never being able to take ourselves, or the vocabulary, or the theory, or the artistic genre we employ entirely seriously. We can no longer (in the postmodernist context) depend on big transcendental knock-down ideas or arguments; we have to rely on each other and on the justificatory outcomes of our local conversations with each other (which include the making of art). The criteria of success will be entirely pragmatic. Vocabularies just succeed one another through history along with their competitors. Some while ago we had 'Neo-Geo painting', now we have the Young British artists and 'Sensation'. Political movements are in no better shape than artistic movements, in this respect. The move from, say, Thatcherism to New Labour is basically a Rortyan change of vocabulary, including all the image-making spin that goes with each government, and not the revelation of new and well-founded political arguments and principles.

If this sort of postmodernist view is accepted, we would indeed have a post-Enlightenment form of liberalism. Maybe this ideal is most obviously appealing in the United States, which is by and large committed to multiculturalism, believes in rights and self-improvement and has a lot of Christian believers within a broadly secular state. It is also an implicitly therapeutic, rather than a philosophical, view – 'let's talk this one through' it says. But of course even this recommendation is no more than a recommendation – and if in true postmodernist fashion this (ironic) form of liberalism were adopted, it would just be one form of life amongst others.

This kind of Rortyan postmodernism may be more difficult to see as a going concern in Britain, France, or Germany, let alone the post-Soviet states, where many of those who come to the dialogue will have non-negotiable even if not *ex hypothesi* obviously indubitable traditional (Marxist, Christian, Islamic, nationalist) positions. But then the sceptical postmodernist rightly says that the problem resides precisely in some people's wholly unjustified certainties. When we ask for 'constructive dialogue' in Northern Ireland we have also in the postmodernist view to ask for some degree of ironic relativism in the main protagonists – and they clearly find this sort of thing hard to come by.

Postmodernist beliefs therefore tend to a multiculturalist pluralism and relativism. In doing so, they can too easily or naively accept what is undoubtedly the case, that most of us in the West now believe we live in societies in which traditional perspectives are fractured. Although we may believe in the *logic* of promise-keeping, can we any longer truly believe in it, in the light of modern realpolitik, in anything like the sense in which Kant and Hume did? These traditional principles, and the alternatives to them, now seem to lack a firm grounding. As John Gray puts it :

The post-modern condition of plural and provisional perspectives, lacking any rational or transcendental ground or unifying world-view, is our own, given to us as an historical fate, and it is idle to pretend otherwise.

John Gray, *Enlightenment's Wake* (1995)

However, as I have tried to indicate above, this condition should be resisted, and not allowed to justify a kind of ironic indifferentism. The claim to superior deconstructive insight depends on notions of truth; the idea that the self is socially constructed in all sorts of different ways does not seem to be able to destroy the idea that people are individuals who make up the unique narrative of their lives, or the idea that the legal rights of individuals need to be defended in the political context by reference to universal principles or ideals, for example those of equality before the law. The beliefs which lead to the public stoning to death of an 'adulterous' woman are not just to be shrugged off as a symptom of 'the way they do things over there' as opposed to 'round here'. It looks as though postmodernist relativism, ironic or not, may really not be much more than a disguised plea for a pluralist tolerance, suitable to the very different kinds of personal, sexual, and ethnic positions which have come to so much prominence – in affluent societies at least – in the postmodernist period. Postmodernist thought has done a great deal to point out and to defend the differences of identity involved here. But they still, as a matter of fact, often lead to bitter conflicts, which need to be resolved by something better than postmodernist principles. For some, homosexuality is against their religion, for others like me it is a matter of taste, with no inherent moral consequences, and for others it involves participation in a culture or way of life which may indeed deserve defence as a whole, but can only be asserted as a matter of right if it doesn't adversely affect the rights of others. Given this, many postmodernist thinkers still need to come to terms with their implied ethical bottom line, which, it seems to me, should be, not an indifferentist relativism, but at best a tolerance of the fact that the values involved in different works of art and different ways of life are, as a matter of undoubted fact, incommensurate, and often in conflict. But tolerance, of the various claims of postmodernists, for example, isn't *ipso facto* relativist at all (though it is often confused with it). Tolerance is a principled willingness to put up with the expression and pursuit of beliefs that you know to be wrong, for the sake of some larger ideal, like freedom of inquiry or the autonomy of others in the construction of their own narrative or identity – provided, I would say, that they don't harm others in the process. But no amount of tolerance or postmodernist scepticism should be allowed to conflict with the ideals expressed, for example, in the United Nations' Universal Declaration of Human Rights (disputable as some of them are) or the Geneva Convention.

As I have argued throughout, postmodernism is a bit like a party manifesto – it is at base a set of beliefs which are not in fact held by all, and are unlikely to reflect the universal condition of men and women in contemporary society. And if we lack an antecedent faith in Marx-plus-Freud, or some other ideology, it is impossible to generalize postmodernist beliefs as diagnosing the 'real' conditions of our existence. (And indeed if we do this we buy into just that kind of larger ideological commitment which it has been the aim of postmodernism to resist.) As Hans Bertens so eloquently puts it:

> Although the omnipresence of the postmodern and its advocates would seem to suggest otherwise, not everybody subscribes to the view that language constitutes rather than represents, reality; that the autonomous and stable subject of modernity has been replaced by a postmodern agent whose identity is largely other-determined and always in process; that meaning has become social and provisional; or that knowledge only counts as such within a given discursive formation, that is a given power structure.
>
> Hans Bertens, *The Idea of the Postmodern* (1994)

Alternatives

The postmodernist critique has worked very well as moral
exhortation, but it has no convincing claim to a unique insight into
the truth of our condition, or to an accurate and complete
description of society. It is therefore important to see postmodernist
ideas and achievements as part of a larger picture of interaction
with other traditions of belief. In all the areas we have looked at,
from philosophy through ethics to artistic activity, there are very
vigorous alternative intellectual traditions outside those promoted
by postmodernists, most notably the Anglo-American liberal
tradition. I am thinking of authors like John Rawls, Joseph Raz,
Michael Sandel, Stuart Hampshire, Amy Guttman, Martha
Nussbaum, Will Kymlicka, John Gray, Ronald Dworkin, Brian
Barry, and Michael Walzer. Richard Rorty seems to be the only
Anglo-American philosopher known to most postmodernist
theorists.

The enduring achievements of postmodernism are therefore likely
to be found not within philosophy or politics, or even in moral
thought, but within the artistic culture. The politics of the
postmodernist era will probably take care of itself as the conditions
under which it became popular change, but what will remain, if
some sense of history and tradition also remains, is a sense of
postmodernism as a cultural phenomenon, which has left us over
the last 30 years of its influence with a canon of major works,
particularly from writers like Abish, Barthelme, Coover, and
DeLillo, and on through the alphabet. A significant number of those
working in the other arts surely have the same status as exemplars
of (some) postmodernist ideas – Joseph Beuys, Christian Boltanski,
Frank Gehry, Philip Glass, Jean-Luc Godard, Robert Rauschenberg,
Richard Rogers, Cindy Sherman, Frank Stella, James Stirling,
Karlheinz Stockhausen, and Wim Wenders among them.

But it is important to remember that in the arts, too, alternative
traditions persist – and for two main reasons – firstly, because

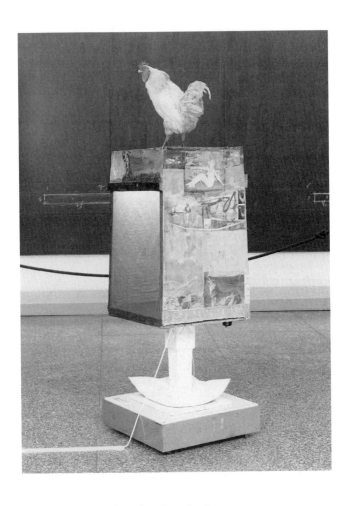

21. *Odalisk* (1955–8) by Robert Rauschenberg.
'Image leads to relativism leads to doubt.' Then what is the bird doing
on top of it all?

modernist traditions continue, and there are many artists who have learned something from postmodernism without being devoted followers of it. Some modernist movements – such as Dada and the use of Duchampian or 'found' objects, constructivism (in its influence on minimalist or colour-field painting) and surrealism (in inspiring the postmodernist's collage of irrationally related images, as for example in Rauschenberg) – seem to have been fairly directly appropriated by postmodernists. Such resemblances and continuities from one period to another are never too difficult to find (there is nothing new under the sun), and the divergences into postmodernism from modernism here are a matter of the different values involved. (Postmodernist surrealism doesn't have the overall theory of Freud to back it up, for example.) And the postmodernist obsession with political difference and with art as politically significant made inevitable an attack upon the (universalizing) claim by modernists that there is pleasure (even if a merely individualist, bourgeois one) to be taken in the immediate or formal properties of works of art. And yet, as I noted earlier, neo-expressionist painting could develop modernist features and thrive in this period, with any obvious or complete allegiance to postmodernist doctrines, and the same goes for traditions of abstraction, and indeed of realism.

Indeed, much of the significant artistic activity of the period since 1945 (and more particularly, for our purposes, since 1970) managed a compromise between modernist and postmodernist ideas. (Of course, there is going to be just as much difficulty in defining 'modernism' in contrast to 'postmodernism' as there is in defining postmodernism itself, and some artists are very difficult to categorize in this respect.) For example, many of the most influential writers, like Milan Kundera, Italo Calvino, Salman Rushdie, John Barth, Julian Barnes, Mario Vargas Llosa, Margaret Atwood, and Umberto Eco, who include in their work many of the concerns of the period, are far from being out-and-out postmodernists. And the same goes for artists like Jennifer Bartlett, Anthony Cragg, Richard Diebenkorn, Eric Fischl, Howard

Hodgkin, David Hockney, Bill Jacklin, and R. B. Kitaj. And many significant composers, such as John Adams, Harrison Birtwhistle, Gyorgy Ligeti, and Witold Lutoslawki, would fit in here.

Hence, for example, the poise of the novels of Umberto Eco (who is himself an important postmodernist theorist), between modern and postmodern. His *The Name of the Rose* (1983) as a detective story seems to thrive on the modernist quest for certainty, but in true postmodernist style 'very little is discovered and the detective is defeated', as Eco declares in the postscript. In the novel William of Baskervile says he arrived at the detection of Jorge 'by mistake'. He thought there was an apocalyptic pattern in the evidence, but it was in fact accidental. He solves many submysteries, but the plot as a whole only through an (ironic) mis-interpretation. But once he is played by Sean Connery in the film of the book, he seems to succeed, because a commercial film no doubt could not afford to bring about too many postmodernist disappointments in its audience.

Many distinguished writers like Eco, have some very obvious postmodernist elements, but they also have a number of more enduring conservative features, which indeed help to place them more nearly at the centre of the culture, as it is very likely to wish to remember itself.

There is plenty of great art outside postmodernism

The staple of many people's artistic experience still lies within a form of liberal realism, which keeps better faith than the postmodernists with the possibility of arriving at the truth, and at a truth where humanitarian as well as political considerations are relevant. Traditionalist liberal novelists like John Updike, Bernard Malamud, Norman Mailer, Saul Bellow, Philip Roth, Heinrich Böll, and Ian McEwan have produced works which are still of immense importance for many people's understanding of contemporary life, as have John Ashbery, Francis Bacon, Ingmar Bergman, Lucian Freud, Gunter Grass, Harold Pinter, François Truffaut, and others in theirs. These are just disputable lists of names, but they are here as a reminder of the ways in which, outside theories, or even explicitly political commitments, we make up canons as individuals, to record and preserve the values that matter for us. Postmodernist art has been a very significant but not obviously predominating part of all this activity.

It has nevertheless been of immense importance in reviving the battle between scepticism and belief, between liberalism and the Marxist left, between strategies for ideological imposition and for the preservation of autonomous identity. It has in these respects borne by far the greatest burden in providing a specification and critique of 'the way we live now' since the 1960s. Its thinkers may have had little purchase upon, and I would guess even less influence upon, the practical everyday activities of professional politicians, though they have had great influence in bringing about an increasingly liberal approach to the 'identity' politics of gender and ethnicity. As cultural critics, they have rightly tended to see political and moral considerations as a quarrel about the legitimacy of particular kinds of *representational*, image-dominated activity.

In this book, I have tried to give an account and a critique of postmodernism, because I believe that the period of its greatest influence is now over. Its founding fathers are in their turn encountering the scepticism of a new generation. That is why I have tried to concentrate above on those postmodernist ideas which I judge to have the longest potential life. For the battles around postmodernism (quite unlike the battles around modernism) have had the distinctive feature that, thanks to the 'rise of theory', they raise perennial philosophical questions. It is this underlying deep dialectic – between reason and scepticism, reality and the image, the political powers of inclusion and exclusion – which is central to postmodernist thought, and it is a dialectic that will continue to engage us for some time to come.

References

In addition to the references and citations I have given throughout the text, the following support and provide background to some of the essential points, topics, and examples discussed in each chapter of this book.

Chapter 1
Frederic Jameson's comments on the Western Bonaventura Hotel in Los Angeles are made in his *Postmodernism, or the Cultural Logic of Late Capitalism* (Verso, 1991), pp. 40, 42, 44.

Chapter 2
Jean-François Lyotard attacks the prevailing grand narratives in *The Postmodern Condition: A Report on Knowledge* (Manchester University Press, 1984).

Edward Said's account of the imposition of the Western imperialist grand narrative onto Oriental societies, along with a discussion of Flaubert's encounter, can be found in his *Orientalism* (Harmondsworth, 1985).

George Lakoff and Mark Johnson explore the influence of Derridean deconstruction in *Metaphors We Live By* (University of Chicago Press, 1980).

The remarks from Alun Munslow are taken from his *Deconstructing History* (Routledge, 1997).

See Deborah Lipstadt, *Denying the Holocaust: The Growing Assault on Truth and Memory* (Penguin, 1993) to get an idea of the consequences of a postmodern approach to history writing.

The 'witch' example is from Richard J. Evans, *In Defence of History* (Granta, 1997) 218f., reporting Diane Purkiss, *The Witch in History: Early Modern and Twentieth Century Representations* (Routledge, 1996), pp. 66–8.

Bruno Latour's comments on Einstein's relativity theory can be found in Noretta Koertge (ed.), *A House Built on Sand* (Oxford University Press, 2000), 12 and 181ff.

Alan Sokal and Jean Bricmont refute the postmodernist 'attack on science' in their *Intellectual Impostures* (Profile, 1998).

Emily Martin's article 'The Egg and the Sperm – How Science Has Constructed a Romance Based on Stereotypical Male-Female Roles' is printed in Evelyn Fox Keller and Helen E. Longino (eds), *Feminism and Science* (Oxford University Press, 1996), p. 103. Scott Gilbert's article is cited by Paul R. Gross in 'Bashful Eggs, Macho Sperm, and Tonypandy' in Koertge op cit., p. 63.

Chapter 3

Foucault's discussion of the episteme takes place in his *The Order of Things: An Archaeology of the Human Sciences* (Tavistock, 1970).

Men, when they get angry and abuse women, seem to find stereotypical, subordinating norms alarmingly available. See George Lakoff, *Women, Fire and Dangerous Things: What Categories Reveal about the Human Mind* (University of Chicago Press, 1987), 380ff.

Chapter 4

Brian McHale presents his views on ontological uncertainty in postmodernist writing in his *Postmodernist Fiction* (Methuen, 1987), pp. 26–43.

For a fuller analysis of the development of postmodernist ideas in music, see Christopher Butler, *After the Wake: An Essay on the Contemporary Avant Garde* (Oxford University Press, 1980), pp. 25–37.

Michael Fried discusses the 'theatricality' of minimalism in *Art and Objecthood* (Chicago University Press, 1998), 148ff.

Rosalind Krauss explores the idea of *re*-production in photography in her *The Originality of the Avant Garde and Other Modernist Myths* (MIT Press, 1985), quote taken from p. 170.

For a more sympathetic account of Bofill's work, see Charles Jencks, *Postmodernism: The New Classicism in Art and Architecture* (Academy, 1987), 258ff.

Chapter 5

For reasons to despair about reason, see John Burrow, *The Crisis of Reason: European Thought, 1848–1914* (Yale University Press, 2000).

The arguments for universalist values have been eloquently put forward by Brian Barry in his *Culture and Equality* (Polity, 2001).

See David Harvey, *The Condition of Postmodernity* (Blackwell, 1980) for a discussion of the influence of the modern media on culture.

Further reading

There are a number of anthologies of postmodernist writings, of which the most committed is Thomas Docherty (ed.), *Postmodernism: A Reader* (Harvester Wheatsheaf, 1993). Ihab Hassan's seminal articles on postmodernism are collected in his *The Postmodern Turn* (Ohio State University Press, 1987). Derrida's thoughts on literature are conveniently brought together in Derek Attridge (ed.), *Jacques Derrida: Acts of Literature* (Routlege, 1992). Steven Connor's *Postmodernist Culture* (Blackwell, 1989) is strongly committed to an eclectic range of postmodernist theories. Charles Jencks's alternative view is neatly summarized in his *What Is Postmodernism?*, revised edn. (Academy, 1996).

For an account of the politics of postmodernism, following Jameson, see Perry Anderson, *The Origins of Postmodernity* (Verso 1998). On nationalist narratives in the postmodern period, looked at from a broadly postmodernist theoretical standpoint, see Elleke Boehmer, *Colonial and Postcolonial Literature* (Oxford University Press, 1995), and Homi Bhabha's anthology, *Nation and Narration* (Routledge, 1990). An excellent early example of the use of Marx, Freud, and deconstruction in literary analysis is Terry Eagleton, *Criticism and Ideology* (NLB, 1976). Useful because they make period contrasts are Patricia Waugh, *Practising Postmodernism/Reading Modernism* (Arnold, 1992) and Peter Brooker, *Modernism/Postmodernism* (Longman, 1992).

The following are critical but also informative about postmodernist tendencies. For an account of the influence of Marx on intellectuals in this period, see J. G. Merquior, *Western Marxism* (Paladin, 1986). The new literary theory encountered surprisingly little published opposition, but see the interestingly entitled *Fraud: Literary Theory and the End of English* by Peter Washington (Fontana, 1989) and Christopher Butler, *Interpretation, Deconstruction, and Ideology* (Clarendon Press, 1984), and, for a general critique, John M. Ellis, *Against Deconstruction* (Princeton University Press, 1989) and Raymond Tallis, *Not Saussure* (Macmillan, 1988). A brilliant account of the relationship of science to political and moral considerations is given by Philip Kitcher in his *Science, Truth and Democracy* (Oxford University Press, 2001). The tendency to the local story attitude of postmodern philosophy has inspired a reply from Thomas Nagel, which defends his view of the value and possibility of objectivity in philosophy and of the abstracting 'view from nowhere' in ethics, expressed in his *The Last Word* (Oxford University Press, 1997).

An influential model for non-linguistic phenomena analysed as text was Roland Barthes, *Système de la mode* (1967; tr. as *The Fashion System*, Hill and Wang, 1983). This approach became common to all 'semiotic' approaches to culture. For a survey, see Robert Hodge and Gunter Kress, *Social Semiotics* (Blackwell, 1988). For a study of the different subject positions open to us within postmodernist theory and the contemporary novel, see Kim Worthington, *Self as Narrative* (Clarendon Press, 1996). For Habermas's critique of postmodernism, see *inter alia* his *The Philosophical Discourse of Modernity* (MIT Press, 1987). Edward Lucie-Smith, *Art Today* (Phaidon, 1995) is an excellent survey of the many current schools of art. An essential resource is to be found in Kristine Stiles and Peter Selz (eds), *Theories and Documents of Contemporary Art* (University of California Press, 1996).

Index

A

Abish, Walter 23, 66–9, 72, 123
abstraction 125
Adams, John 76, 84, 85, 89, 126
Adès, Thomas 75
advertising 114
Africano, Nicholas 107
Althusser, Louis 6
Andre, Carl 1–2, 5, 82
Archipenko, Alexander 84
architecture 89–91
Ashbery, John 126
Asher, Michael 92
Atwood, Margaret 125
Auden, W. H. 55
Auster, Paul 69
author, death of the 23–4

B

Bach, Johann Sebastian 74
Bacon, Francis 126
Bad Writing Contest 9–10
Barnes, Julian 71–2, 73, 125
Barry, Brian 123
Barry, Robert 81
Barth, John 52–3, 125
Barthelme, Donald 23, 69, 123
Barthes, Roland
  art 66
  copying, art as 68
  death of the author 23–4
  difference, politics of 58
  self and identity 55
  seventeenth-century French
    literature 9
  stereotypes 68
  'text of bliss' 68
  textualizing view of the
    world 105
  theory, rise of 6, 7
  truth, confidence in 111
Bartlett, Jennifer 107, 125
Baselitz, Georg 106
Bataille, George 6
Baudrillard, Jean 40, 112–14
Beckett, Samuel 6, 69, 74
Bellow, Saul 52, 126
Belsey, Catherine 53
Benglis, Lynda 94–5
Benhabib, Seyla 29, 51, 57, 58
Bergman, Ingmar 126
Berio, Luciano 74
Bertens, Hans 122
Beuys, Joseph 6, 123
Bhabha, Homi 10
Birtwhistle, Harrison 75, 126
Bofill, Ricardo 91
Böll, Heinrich 126
Boltanski, Christian 123
Boulez, Pierre 6, 74, 76, 84
Bowie, David 64
Brancusi, Constantin 84
Braque, Georges 76
Brecht, Bertolt 6, 73
Bricmont, Jean 39–40
Brown, Denise Scott 89–91
Bruckner, Anton 76
Buchloh, Benjamin 102

C

Cage, John 75
Calvino, Italo 125
Camus, Albert 6, 7

Caro, Anthony 2, 82
  Early One Morning 82
Carter, Angela 56
Chia, Sandro 106
Chicago, Judy, *The Dinner
  Party* 95–7
Cixous, Helene 97
Clemente, Francisco 106
Close, Chuck 80
Colescott, Robert 107
  *Grandma and the
  Frenchman (Identity
  Crisis)* 108
Colet, Louise 16
conceptualism 3, 78–85
Connery, Sean 126
Connor, Steven 88
Constitution of the United
  States 13–14
constructivism 125
consumerism 66, 118
Cook, Peter 44
Coover, Robert 6, 23, 69, 94,
  123
Cragg, Anthony 125
Craig-Martin, Michael, *An
  Oak Tree* 82–4
Creed, Martin 2
Crimp, Douglas 87, 108–9
criticism, function of 102
Crowther, Paul 78–81
Cubism 76, 84
cultural studies movement 116
Currie, Peter 52

D

Dada 125
Davenport, Guy 69

death of the author
  23–4
Debussy, Claude 74
deconstruction 7, 16–19
  conceptualism 81
  death of the author 24
  difference, politics of
    58
  history 36
  metaphor 25–8
  music 76
  scepticism and ideology 28,
    31
  science 40
  signs as systems 21
  text 21–3
DeLillo, Don 3, 123
de Man, Paul 28, 30
Derrida, Jacques
  art 66
  deconstruction 16, 17, 24
  difference, politics of 57, 58
  grand narratives, resisting
    15
  metaphor 25
  political position 105
  Saussure's work 8
  scepticism and ideology 28,
    29, 30, 32
  self and identity 51, 56
  signs as systems 19–20, 21
  style, Foucault's views 9
  theory, rise of 6, 7
  words, power of 47
de Saussure, Ferdinand 8
Diamond, Jessica 103
Diebenkorn, Richard 125
differance 19, 23, 94
difference, politics of 56–61

discourse and power 44,
     92–101
  self and identity 50–1, 56
  words, power of 56–9
Disneyland 112–13
Doctorow, E. L. 56, 69
Duchamp, Marcel 2, 66, 125
Dworkin, Ronald 123

E

Eagleton, Terry 49
Eco, Umberto 32, 125, 126
egg and sperm controversy
     41–2, 57
Einstein, Albert 37
Eliot, George 18, 19, 20, 24
Eno, Brian 64
Epstein, Jacob 5
Estes, Richard 80
  Drugs 79
ethics 121–2
Euhemerism 16
Evan, Walker 88
Evans, Richard 36

F

Faulkner, William 70, 73
Federman, Ray 23
  Take It or Leave It: A Novel
     22
feminism
  difference, politics of 57–8
  discourse and power 95–101
  history, rewriting 34
  male gaze 86
  politics, art as 103
Figes, Orlando 34
Fischl, Eric 64, 106, 125

Fitkin, Graham 84
Flack, Audrey 80
Flaubert, Gustave 6, 16
Forster, E. M. 16, 20
Foucault, Michel
  art 66
  death of the author 23
  on Derrida's style 9
  difference, politics of 58, 60,
     61
  discourse and power 92
  grand narratives, resisting 16
  self and identity 50, 51
  theory, rise of 6, 7
  unreal images 112
  words, power of 45–6, 47,
     48–9
'found' objects 125
Fowles, John, *The French
     Lieutenant's Woman*
     70–1, 73
Freud, Lucian 126
Freud, Sigmund 29–30, 42, 97,
     115, 125
Freudianism 13, 20, 51, 114
Fried, Michael 82, 83
Fuentes, Carlos 69

G

Gehry, Frank 123
Geneva Convention 122
Gentileschi, Artemisia 97
Ghirardo, Diane 90
Gilbert, Scott 41
Glass, Philip 64, 76, 84, 123
Godard, Jean-Luc 5, 31, 73,
     123
Godfrey, Tony 84

grand narratives, resisting 13–16
Grass, Gunter 57, 126
Gray, John 120–1, 123
Gross, Paul 42
Guttman, Amy 123

H

Haacke, Hans 92, 102, 104
Habermas, Jürgen 61
Hampshire, Stuart 123
Hanem, Kuchuk 16
Hanson, Duane 80
Hartman, Geoffrey 28
Harvey, David 117
Hassan, Ihab 5
Heidegger, Martin 6, 87
Henze, Hans Werner 76, 84
historiographical metafiction 70–3
history, rewriting 32–6, 70–3
Hockney, David 126
Hodgkin, Howard 126
Hopkins, David 97
Hughes, Robert 59, 103–4
Hume, David 120
Hutcheon, Linda 52, 87, 93
Huyssen, Andreas 64
hyperrealization 114

I

identity 50–6, 57–9, 121
ideology 28–32
Imagination, Romantic view of 12
Immendorff, Jorg 106
Impressionism 76
Internet 117

intertextuality 24, 31–2, 85, 89
irony, postmodernist 118–19, 120–1
Izenour, Steven 89

J

Jacklin, Bill 126
Jameson, Frederic 3, 31, 87, 110, 111–12
Jencks, Charles 64, 89
JFK 112
Johns, Jasper, *Fool's House* 63
Johnson, Mark 25
Joyce, James 5, 32, 70, 73
Just, E. E. 42
justice 115

K

Kant, Immanuel 120
Kantianism 51, 55, 59
Kelly, Mary 64
Kesey, Ken 48
Kiefer, Anselm 64, 80, 106
King, Martin Luther 74
Kitaj, R. B. 126
Koons, Jeff 66
    New Hoover Quadraflex 65
Krauss, Rosalind 87
Kruger, Barbara 99–100, 102
Kundera, Milan 111, 125
Kymlicka, Will 123

L

Laing, R. D. 48
Lakoff, George 25
Lascaux Caves 114
Latour, Bruno 37

Le Corbusier 77, 92
Levine, Sherrie 87–8
Lévi-Strauss, Claude 74
Ligeti, Gyorgy 75, 126
Lutoslawski, Witold 126
Lyotard, Jean-François 28, 29,
    49, 60, 62
  grand narratives, resisting
    13, 14, 15
Lysenkoism 39

M

McEwan, Ian 126
McHale, Brian 69
McLuhan, Marshall 3
Madonna 64–6
magic realist fiction 69
Mahler, Gustav 74
Mailer, Norman 126
Malamud, Bernard 126
Mallarmé, Stephane 6, 70
Man, Paul de 28, 30
Manet, Edouard 86
Mapplethorpe scandal 104
Martin, Emily 41
Marx, Karl 2, 42
  difference, politics of 59
  scepticism and ideology 29,
    30
  theory, rise of 7
  unreal images 115
  words, power of 49
Marxism 45, 60, 103, 111, 114
  grand narratives, resisting
    13, 14
master narratives, resisting
    13–16
Matisse, Henri 5

media 110–11, 114–15, 117
mesmerism 12
metanarratives, resisting
    13–16
metaphor 24–8
Mies van der Rohe, Ludwig 5
Miller, Hillis 28, 30
minimalism 1, 3, 81–5
modernism
  architecture 89
  art 64, 66, 77
  conceptualism 80, 81–3
  discourse and power 94
  formalism 105
  metanarratives 62, 64
  music 74
  novels 70, 73
  postmodernism's relation to
    5, 86–9, 125
  postmodernist criticisms 6
  sensory overload 117
  unreal images 111–12
Monet, Claude 107
Morley, Malcolm, *SS
    Amsterdam in Front of
    Rotterdam* 77, 78–80
Morris, Robert 82
Mulvey, Laura 47
Munslow, Alun 33, 36
Murdoch, Iris 51–2
Murray, Elizabeth 107
  Her Story 107
music 73–6
  minimalism 84–5

N

Nabokov, Vladimir 69
Nagel, Thomas 51

Index

National Gallery, Sainsbury Wing, London 89–91
neo-expressionism 106–9, 125
Neue Staatsgallerie, Stuttgart 91
'new novel' 69
Nietzsche, Friedrich 6, 16, 24, 112
Nono, Luigi 76
novels 68–73
Nussbaum, Martha 123
Nyman, Michael 84

O

October group 107–9
opera 75–6
Oppenheimer, Robert 39
Orwell, George *1984* 48

P

Penck, P. A. R. 106
Philosophy and Literature 10
photography 87–8, 93–4, 100–1
Picasso, Pablo 76
Pinter, Harold 126
Plato 24, 31
Plutarch 33
political art 102–9
Portman, Jon, Westin Bonaventura Hotel, LA 3, 4
Post-Impressionism 76
poststructuralist theory 7
power and discourse 44, 92–102
  self and identity 50–1, 56
  words, power of 56–9

Prince, Richard 87
Proust, Marcel 6
Purkiss, Diane 36
Pynchon, Thomas 3, 69

R

Rauschenberg, Robert 5, 6, 123, 125
  Odalisk 124
Ravel, Maurice 74
Rawls, John 10, 51, 123
Raz, Joseph 123
Reich, Riley 84
Renoir, Jean 5
Robbe-Grillet, Alain 5, 6, 7, 69, 94
Rodin, Auguste 2
Rogers, Richard 123
Rorty, Richard 118–19, 120, 123
Rose, Barbara 107
Rosler, Martha 95
Roth, Philip 52, 126
Rushdie, Salman 14, 52, 56–7, 111, 125
Ryle, Gilbert 10

S

Said, Edward 15–16
Sainsbury Wing, National Gallery, London 89–91
Salle, David 64, 75, 106
Salt, John 80
Sandel, Michael 123
Sartre, Jean-Paul 6
Saussure, Ferdinand de 8
scepticism 28–32, 61
Schama, Simon 34

Schindler's List 103
Schnabel, Julian 75, 106
Schneeman, Carolee, *Interior Scroll* 97, 98
Schnittke, Alfred 75
Schoenberg, Arnold 74, 76, 85
Schopenhauer, Arthur 97
Schwarz, K. Robert 85
science, attacking 37–42
Scott Brown, Denise 89–90
Searle, John 8–9
self 50–6, 57–9, 121
Seurat, Georges 93
Shakespeare, William 33, 49
Sherman, Cindy 87, 123
    #228 97–9
    Untitled Film Stills 53–5
Shostakovich, Dmitri Dmitrievich 75
signs as systems 19–21, 111–12, 114, 118
Silverman, Gilbert 104
Simpson, O. J. 115
Smith, David 84
social construction theories 58
Social Text 40
Sokal, Alan 39–40
Sollers, Philippe 7
Sontag, Susan 5
sperm and egg controversy 41–2, 57
Spielberg, Steven 103
Stella, Frank 123
Stirling, James 91, 123
Stockhausen, Karlheinz 5, 6, 84, 123
Stone, Oliver 3, 112
Stravinsky, Igor 5, 76
surrealism 10–11, 77, 125

T

Takemitsu, Toru 75
television 110–11, 117
Tennyson, Alfred, Lord 26–7, 29
text, playing with the 21–3
textualizing view of the world 105–6
Theatre of Abraxis 91, 92
theory
    and art 76–8
    rise of 5–8
Thomas, Keith 36
tolerance 121–2
Torke, Michael 84
Toselli Gallery, Milan 92
translation, problems with 8–11
Truffaut, François 126
truth, confidence in 110–11
Turnage, Mark-Antony 75

U

United Nations' Declaration on Human Rights 122
Updike, John 52, 126

V

Van Gogh, Vincent 87
Vargas Llosa, Mario 125
Venturi, Robert 5, 89–91
vocal music 75–6

W

Wagner, Richard 85
Wall, Jeff 86

Index

Walzer, Michael 123
Warhol, Andy 87
Waugh, Patricia 72
Weber, Max 60
Wenders, Wim 123
Westin Bonaventura Hotel, LA 3, 4
Weston, Edward 87–8

White, Hayden 33, 70
Wilding, Faith 95
Wilson, Angus 51
Wilson, Robert 76
Wittgenstein, Ludwig 8, 17
Wood, Paul 93, 99
words, power of 45–50